Hanratty
The Inconvenient Truth

By
Alan Razen

Copyright

First Edition (June 2014)

Printed by CreateSpace, An Amazon.com Company
Available on Kindle and other devices

2

Contents

Preface

The "A6 Murder" case is one of the most notorious of British legal history. James Hanratty was convicted and then executed on the 4th April 1962. Even before the execution, controversy was raging and a strong pro-Hanratty alliance had already formed determined to prove Hanratty's innocence. That controversy still continues today, though the principal protagonists are now confined (largely) to his immediate family; in fact, the vast majority of people connected to this case are now deceased.

In 2001, DNA analysis seemed to convincingly prove Hanratty's guilt, yet there are those that still cling to the belief that he was innocent. Their conviction should not surprise us though: after 50 years of campaigning, there is probably nothing that could shake their deeply entrenched faith in James Hanratty. So despite the damning nature of this DNA evidence, the family refuse to accept its authenticity, claiming that it must be the result of contamination.

The cornerstone of the British legal system has always been that no one should be convicted if there is a *reasonable doubt* in determining their guilt. What constitutes a reasonable doubt though is open to debate and will vary from case to case, and even DNA evidence is not necessarily definitive. As the science of DNA profiling has advanced, so has the sensitivity of the analytical methods, to the extent that only a few cells are required to extract sufficient material to provide a viable sample, from which accurate and comprehensive information can be derived. Samples from tissues that are thousands of years old can now yield reliable results. However, the older and/or more insubstantial the sample, the greater the risk of contamination becomes; so the irony of the availability of this advanced forensic tool has been to reduce confidence in DNA profiling in general. This has more to do with ignorance of the process, than any genuine justification. Certainly, DNA evidence should always be evaluated according to the particular merits of the case in question; the exact circumstances pertaining to the nature and collection of a given sample and any potential means or likelihood of contamination should be duly considered in assessing the veracity of any particular DNA profiling result, while the precision achieved in matching and associated potential probability of obtaining that specific degree of match should be disclosed. But, provided rigorous standards are maintained – as should be applied to all criminal case evidence – then there is no reason not to accept the resultant conclusions that may be drawn.

What it is important to realise is that in any criminal case, there is never such a thing as absolute certainty. A clear cut verdict will only ever be accomplished by assessing what level of probability of guilt is acceptable to those involved, whether a jury or judge(s). Therefore, *reasonable doubt* equates to a non-specific level of probability, i.e. a *sufficiently* small level of uncertainty in a defendant's guilt is what is required to convict them. DNA profiling evidence can profoundly affect the probability of establishing guilt or innocence; whether a given conclusion is unexpected, (perhaps *apparently* inconceivable,) is irrelevant, provided that there is no other substantially contradictory evidence. However, in the future it may be necessary to treat DNA evidence with greater caution, with the advent of the ability to generate artificial DNA. This is only a very recent development, so is not relevant to this case.

The original "A6 Murder" trial was an undoubted travesty. The prosecution case was weak and depended on disputable circumstantial evidence, dubious witness testimony and a singular lack of motive; there is also reason to suspect (despite there being no hard evidence to support the assertion) that both evidence and witnesses were interfered with by the investigating police officers. Unfortunately, Hanratty's defence team, who should have ripped several gaping holes in the prosecution case, instead spent an inordinate amount of time nit-picking and desperately attempting to discredit evidence, a great deal of which simply did not warrant serious consideration; not dismissing this out of hand may actually have added credence to it, while they incomprehensibly failed to sufficiently highlight a number of key deficiencies

/discrepancies of the case. That said, there is little doubt that the prosecution acted unprofessionally: they did not disclose everything they should have to the defence (and didn't present their *own* case as well as they perhaps could have done). In fairness, though, the defence had a difficult job on their hands and were obliged to examine all the details of a prosecution case that was brimming with trivia and questionable sources; it was further hampered by a multitude of red herrings. But what remains more shocking and extraordinary is that the jury returned a unanimous guilty verdict. Of course, what no one had access to then was the DNA evidence.

There are surely few who would regard the Hanratty murder trial as anything other than a dreadful miscarriage of justice. With the evidence available at that time, he should have been acquitted and at the very least, the lack of certainty apparent from that evidence should have prompted the judge to commute the sentence to life imprisonment – whereupon, Hanratty would of had a much better opportunity to mount a successful appeal. As it was, there was no reprieve for Hanratty and his appeal, (also inconceivably – given the outcry at the time –) was refused. In the aftermath of his execution, there was a sustained campaign to clear his name that continued intensely for decades, prompting along the way a number of people (some quite prominent) to produce supportive literature that examined the details of the case, including in 1997 an important reinvestigatory work which included hitherto undisclosed police records. One would be very hard pressed to find a dissenting voice amidst this abundance of pro-Hanratty propaganda. When the original DNA analysis was conducted in 1999, everyone (including the police) expected the result to exonerate Hanratty, but it was inconclusive – however, this had relied on familial DNA for matching to Hanratty. Consequently, in 2000, Hanratty's corpse was exhumed to obtain his own DNA and the subsequent analyses indicated Hanratty's guilt was proven "beyond doubt". Indeed, the subsequent Court of Appeal, which considered every aspect of the case, including the potential for DNA contamination, concluded that there was certain proof of guilt.

Having taken an interest in this case in the 1970's following publication of Paul Foot's contemporarily definitive book ['Who Killed Hanratty?'], I had long held the opinion that Hanratty was wrongfully executed and very probably innocent. When the DNA evidence seemed to prove otherwise, I was initially surprised, *but* not entirely. The biggest issue with this case is that after the trial the only voice to be found on the subject derives from the pro-Hanratty lobby. Paul Foot's book is commendable, but ultimately biased. There was always some thread of a case against Hanratty, albeit exceedingly flimsy; but when combined with the DNA "proof", a whole new complexion can be put upon it. Following some heated discussions with one of my own family members with regard to the implications of the DNA evidence – which they disputed – I decided to revisit this case. In doing so, I sought a more recent examination of the case to Paul Foot's 1973 tome and found this in the form of Bob Woffinden's 1997 publication 'Hanratty: The Final Verdict'. Though this is another pro-Hanratty contribution, it doesn't hide the facts, even where they seem to implicate or weaken Hanratty's case and was written prior to the DNA profiling, so is not tainted by that. Moreover, it is an authoritative and thorough review of all of the available information, and as such, can be regarded as definitive as it is possible to get within the confines of popular literature. Of course, its purpose was to exonerate Hanratty and so determinedly (albeit with earnest integrity) seeks to subvert any possible case that could be made against Hanratty. I therefore resolved that if I could formulate a reasonable case against Hanratty using this book as my source, then that would reinforce any conclusions of his guilt that might now be arrived at.

Given that it has been some years since Hanratty's mother passed away, I believe it is time that the original "A6 Murder" case was re-evaluated from the perspective that Hanratty was probably guilty, as opposed to the premise of most previous assessments that presumed Hanratty to be innocent. The DNA evidence and Appeal verdict should have drawn a final veil over this case, but it is still disputed. [A 2002 Channel 4 programme did re-examine the case from the perspective of proving Hanratty's guilt, but this passed largely unnoticed.]

This book attempts to objectively re-evaluate the key elements of the original evidence on the basis that the 2001 DNA analysis is valid (and Hanratty must therefore be guilty) to determine whether a more robust case could have been constructed against him, regardless of whether that would be enough to convict in a modern court in the absence of the DNA evidence – I also argue the case for accepting the virtues of that evidence, despite the potential for contamination and degradation of the samples. I will also present a variety of speculative conclusions. It is unfortunately impossible not to concede to some subjectivity, as the evidence that was originally collated is far from comprehensive and many avenues of interest from both sides of the argument remain uninvestigated, while separating the evidential wheat from the chaff is one of the major challenges in tackling this case and consequently leads to excluding a lot of (mostly tenuous) material. Moreover, the original prosecution, defence and all subsequent prominent examinations of the case involve the necessity to speculate in order to arrive at a meaningful conclusion. That is what makes this case so fascinating.

For the record, I would like to emphasise that I intend no disrespect to either Hanratty's family or any of the many people who have campaigned on his behalf: they remain entitled to their opinion. As already highlighted, appraising criminal guilt is always a matter of weighing-up probabilities and consequently will always be subject to individual opinion. The nature of this case is such that it is unlikely that it will ever be satisfactorily closed; even within this book, there is a suggestion of a possible scenario whereby Hanratty could still be innocent. I will no doubt be accused of skewing the evidence in directions that suit my hypotheses, but I would proffer no more than anyone else has ever done.

Chapter One

Opportunity

On the 22nd of August 1961 Michael Gregsten and Valerie Storie were sitting in a Morris Minor parked inside the entrance to a cornfield (off the secluded Marsh Lane) in Dorney Reach, Buckinghamshire. At around 9.45 pm they were interrupted by a man brandishing a .38 revolver. Thus begun an extraordinary episode that lasted approximately six hours, concluding in another secluded spot known as Deadman's Hill in a lab-by off the A6 (near Clophill in Bedfordshire) by which time Gregsten had been shot dead, while Storie had been raped and left for dead after also being shot a number of times – resulting in her being paralysed for the rest of her life.

The gunman's motive to this day remains a mystery; the rape of Storie was *possibly* incidental to the abduction, an opportunistic event arising from the gunman most likely having already decided to kill her. The only apparent purpose in the killer's actions would seem to be to hitch a ride, but (on the face of it) this explanation makes little sense of a very convoluted and staggered journey through Slough and the outskirts of London [via Hayes and Harrow] onto Watford, Aldenham, St. Albans and eventually to Luton, before heading out to Barton-le-Clay, Silsoe and finally, Clophill.

However, after dispensing with Gregsten and Storie, it is known that the gunman drove back into the London suburbs from a reliable sighting of the vehicle in Ilford at around 7 am and was last seen heading into Redbridge, where the car was recovered in the early evening [about 6.30 pm] of the 23rd August. Prior to this bizarre journey, the gunman had behaved strangely indecisive: it was about an hour before he decided to leave the cornfield, which he had forced them to drive further into. He may have been spooked by the activities of a local resident at a cottage adjoining the field some distance away, though his decision to set off was given as a wish to obtain food – and then return to the field, which of course they never did.

During the trial, a great deal was made of what was said by the gunman throughout the six hour abduction. In particular, his cockney accent, use of the word 'kip', various ramblings about his criminal history, some personal details and an apparent familiarity with East London. Interestingly, some of the things he said were so specific that were they all true, it should have been a relatively simple matter for the police to identify him, when in fact they didn't have the first clue. One of the primary thrusts of the prosecution case was to demonstrate as many comparisons with Hanratty as they possibly could, yet most were sufficiently non-specific and/or ambiguous that they could have been applied to a wide swathe of the male London population – at the very least. This is one of the facets of the prosecution case that the defence should have ridiculed as utterly meaningless. Though he might conceivably have made the odd Freudian slip, the only thing that could be reasonably construed was the gunman's perceived affinity with East London – though even this is disputed to some extent. The subsequent general conclusion has to be that what the gunman imparted was largely invention, either intended to mislead, scare or "impress". But there is an important conclusion to be drawn from this: if the gunman always intended to kill Gregsten and Storie, there would be no need to create a smokescreen of lies; on the other hand, if he was telling essentially the truth, he was unlikely to have been neither Hanratty, nor any other potential suspect or known offender. Therefore, on balance of probability it would be reasonable to deduce that the gunman did not originally set out to kill anyone. Certainly Storie's testimony appears to support that notion and that killing Gregsten was more accident than intention; though it can't be discounted that he had been contemplating it and just waiting for an excuse to justify himself, one would still be inclined to believe that this was never the intended purpose of the kidnap. Which raises the important question: what was the purpose?

The cornfield at Dorney Reach is (even today) a fairly remote location. Given Storie's impression of the gunman that he was immaculately dressed, it seems unlikely that he could have walked across the cornfield and much more likely that he had arrived at the scene via the road. Unfortunately, the police enquiries did not uncover a single witness to verify that anyone had been seen walking along the relevant roads at around that time. In fact, one has to wonder what anyone, other than a local, would have been doing walking in that area in the late evening, when it was nearly dark. And incidentally, there has never been any indication that the crime was committed by someone local to Dorney Reach. Assuming that he hadn't been sleeping rough for days (possibly on the run, as he claimed) *and* possibly trudged across an unharvested cornfield, there is no obvious reason why the gunman would have been in that location nor been drawn to the parked vehicle in order to terrorise and abduct the occupants. Moreover, Hanratty was nothing more than a common burglar with no previously known violent tendencies. It is difficult to imagine that if Hanratty was the gunman he would have committed this random crime spontaneously while going about his normal criminal activities, and it is difficult to imagine why even he would have been wandering along that particular road, anyway. Everything about this case implies some form of *targeted* attack. This conclusion seems to be what the prosecution were implying in order to counter Hanratty's alibi; yet, despite the fact the whole prosecution premise was that this was a planned event, no motive was ever established, nor anyone else implicated. Hanratty had no connection to Gregsten or

Storie and therefore no personal reason to target them. Surprisingly, the defence did not seize upon this deficiency in their case and failed to force the prosecution to present some evidence to support their rationale. Why for example, if they believed this to be a planned attack, were they not seeking any co-conspirators that surely that rationale would have required? There was never any evidence known to have been uncovered that would support this idea and (most significantly) neither was there an investigation into what would have been the manifestly implicit wider conspiracy. If Hanratty was the gunman, it appears inexplicable that he would have acted completely in isolation.

In reality, there *was* a known potential motive for an attack on Gregsten and Storie, because Gregsten was married (with children) and they were having an illicit affair. This was not disclosed in court, undoubtedly to protect Storie's reputation and sensibilities: she had after all been raped and crippled. On the face of it, this detail was irrelevant to the committal of the crime anyhow, *if* the choice of victims were random, even assuming the perpetrator had intended to commit an attack of this nature; however, the suggestion that anyone would go to the lengths implied by the prosecution case to construct the alibi Hanratty was presenting, just reeks of absurdity.

Technically, the withholding of the details of the affair was reprehensible, *but* perhaps entirely comprehendible, particularly when bearing in mind this was the early 1960's – such behaviour was scorned upon. Nonetheless this was not an excuse for the defence in what was a capital crime: they really should have highlighted the discrepancies, even if they were unaware of the affair – though it beggars belief that they could be that naive, and it may be that they were not. Though there is not a shred of evidence to support the proposition, I would suggest that there is the possibility that the defence either feared, suspected or knew that Hanratty was guilty and that he had been hired to frighten Gregsten and Storie into ending their affair; therefore, to instigate an investigation into a conspiracy might actually be detrimental to Hanratty and if true would not save him from the gallows. Equally, the police and prosecution may have chosen to suppress their suspicion of a conspiracy on the basis that pursuit of such a line of enquiry was not in the public interest: any co-conspirators may have acted illegally, but it is unimaginable that rape and murder were ever part of the plan, and considering that they were likely connected to Gregsten and/or Storie, it may have been decided that they had suffered enough already. Unethical though this response would have been, it would certainly be understandable.

In order to assess whether it was possible for Hanratty to have committed this crime, we must examine his alibi in detail. He insisted that he had gone to Liverpool late morning on the day of the murder with the purpose of meeting some criminal contacts who were to 'fence' some stolen jewellery and a watch. He had purportedly taken a train from Euston station (probably) at 11.55 [it was never definitively established]; he claimed that he arrived in Liverpool at about 3.30 pm. He then later met up with three criminal associates and stayed at the flat of one of them [Terry McNally] for three days. Unfortunately, Hanratty had initially been unwilling to provide any details of these people or their addresses; he claimed that they had subsequently disowned him when he became associated with the murder and would not help him anyway. This of course was of little help to the police or Hanratty's case, though it is credible that these crooks would be unwilling to get involved. However, Hanratty did later provide information relating to the identity and locations of these individuals, also claiming that Terry McNally had sold some jewellery for him on the 24th of August. Then, during the trial, he amended his alibi: he now claimed that having been unable to locate his associates and not sold any jewellery, he departed Liverpool at 6 pm by bus and arrived in Rhyl (in Wales) at about 8.20 pm on the 22nd of August (where he stayed for two nights), making it impossible for him to have been at Dorney Reach by 9.45 pm.

What is known for certain is that Hanratty sent a telegram from Liverpool at 8.40 pm on the 24th August to Charles France – Hanratty's friend and criminal associate – stating that he would be returning early on Friday "for business". He had given his name and address as *Mr.P.Ryan, Imperial Hotel, Russell Square, London* and signed it 'Jim' [*Jim(my) Ryan* was an alias Hanratty sometimes used]. The prosecution posited that this was sent in order to complete Hanratty's alibi; the defence argued that because he had given a London address, this would not be consistent with the idea that the telegram was sent deliberately as means to place him in Liverpool. This is one of the many irrelevancies that clouded the case: placing himself in Liverpool late on the 24th did not prove he was in Liverpool or Rhyl on the evening of the 22nd and he could certainly have returned to Liverpool on the 23rd or 24th after committing the crime. What is more, Hanratty always claimed that France showed him this telegram when he arrived at his home at around 8.45 am on the 25th *and* that the postman had just delivered it – which begs the question: why *did* he bother sending it? However, though this did not help the case much, one way or the other, he was able to provide some details of witnesses he had spoken to in Liverpool on the 22nd. The most reliable was Olive Dunwoodie who was serving in a sweetshop where Hanratty stopped to ask directions: she recalled him vividly and confirmed that it had to have been on either the 21st or 22nd of August (between 3.30 and 4 pm), because these were the only days during the relevant period that she had been there – this was indisputable. Unfortunately for Hanratty, she was adamant it had been on the 21st. Her reasoning was mainly to do with the presence of 13-year-old Barbara Ford, who was also serving on the 21st, but not the 22nd. As with most things in this case, it wasn't quite that straightforward: Barbara did have some recollection of Hanratty, but couldn't remember exactly when (albeit she favoured the 21st) and it transpired that Barbara had visited the shop on the 22nd, possibly serving for a period. Furthermore, a delivery man seemed to corroborate Dunwoodie, though it was later discovered that he too could have been mistaken about the day. Given that these recollections were made months after the actual events, there was clearly room for error.

As far as the Rhyl part of Hanratty's alibi goes, there was corroboration by the landlady [Grace Jones] of the guest house where he claimed to have stayed on the night of the 22nd and 23rd, to the extent that she identified him as having been there during the week of 19-26th of August; he also had accurately described various aspects of the residence that supported him having been there. Another good witness placed him in Rhyl High Street on the morning of the 23rd. There were a number of other witnesses who believed that they had seen Hanratty in Rhyl on 22nd (some very persuasive), but these were never fully investigated – a serious failure on the part of the police. This information came late on in the trial and Grace Jones' evidence was tainted by the suggestion of collusion by no less than a member of the jury who had brought the matter to the courts' attention.

The biggest problem with witness evidence when it is based on recalling events from months in the past that they would not have known they needed to remember at the time is that it is notoriously unreliable. Regardless of the honesty or best intentions of a witness, people can and do invariably make genuine mistakes about important details. So we must treat all of this evidence with caution. Moreover, people can be prone to lying, exaggeration, embellishment, attention seeking and may be attracted by the notoriety of a high profile murder case.

There is one last significant piece of witness evidence relating to Hanratty's alibi: Charles France, his wife and daughter all gave evidence which indicated that Hanratty had been at the France's flat on the 21st and did not leave until 7 pm. Hanratty made a point about this during cross-examination, as it contradicted the prosecution's theory that he had gone to Liverpool on the 21st so as to create a false alibi for the 22nd. Hanratty's defence should have made a meal of this, not least of all because the France's were witnesses for the prosecution! The pro-Hanratty lobby have always implied that the France's had been coerced by the police into giving distorted evidence against Hanratty. Whatever the truth, it seems unlikely that they would have lied about this particular detail.

There is also a critical fact that seems to have been overlooked by the prosecution in relation to Hanratty's alibi. This relates to his indisputable stay at the Vienna Hotel, Maida

Vale on the night of the 21st. The irrefutable fact is that he arrived there between 9 and 11 pm. If Hanratty had been in Liverpool that afternoon, the time scale issue would have applied equally in explaining how he could have achieved this as it did to the 22nd. Basically, the prosecution were trying to have their cake and eat it, instead of addressing the real issue of whether he could have made it back from Liverpool within a minimal window of time. The defence did question the practicality of doing this, to which the officer in charge of the investigation [Detective Superintendent Basil Acott] glibly suggested that he could have caught an air flight. This is probably one of the most ludicrous assertions made during the whole trial: Hanratty was just simply not the sort of person who travelled by aircraft in 1961 and there certainly wasn't any evidence to support it.

It is difficult to know what to make of all this conflicting information, but obviously Hanratty's whereabouts on the 21st/22nd of August were critical to the both sides of the case. In regard to the Rhyl alibi, I believe it must be rejected, principally because there is no logical reason for Hanratty to have withheld this until after the trial was well under way – and he probably realised he was going to lose. I would suggest that he did go to Rhyl (via Liverpool) much as he described except that it was on the 23rd (not the 22nd) following abandonment of the Morris Minor in Redbridge, for the purposes of lying low – rather than to create a possible false alibi as insisted by the prosecution. Personally, I believe it is implausible that Hanratty went to Liverpool or Rhyl in order to facilitate false alibis. What is also implausible though is the pro-Hanratty lobby's contention that Hanratty withheld this information in order to save face with his criminal associates, on the basis that he was embarrassed by the lack of success in his jaunt to Liverpool. Hanratty himself insisted the reason was his difficulty in recalling verifiable details about it, which in itself is suspect considering the detail he recalled in relation to his time in Liverpool. Bearing in mind that his life was at stake, it seems illogical to persist with an alibi that was false and therefore was never going to be proven, when he had a perfectly good *supposedly* real alibi that at least had the potential to be verified and did not rest on the word of dubious criminal witnesses. The reason therefore for creating the original false alibi can only be because he was guilty and simply hadn't yet constructed the false Rhyl alibi. However, from the perspective of the Rhyl being forwarded as a false alibi, it very nearly worked. I think it is fair to say that if defendants are allowed to change their story until they come up with something that is *allegedly* corroborated by someone, then *no one* would ever be convicted.

Without the Rhyl alibi, what this all boils down to isn't whether Hanratty was in Liverpool on the 21st or the 22nd, but whether it is possible and plausible for him to have returned from Liverpool on the 22nd in time to initiate the crime in Dorney Reach, because if he was in Liverpool on the 21st, then his whereabouts on the 22nd would be

24

unknown and he could easily [in theory, at least] be placed at the scene of the crime. So, if we assume that he did indeed visit Liverpool on the 22nd, how and why did he finish up at Dorney Reach within a maximum of six hours? It does not seem credible that he would have taken that journey if he had always intended to return after just one or two hours. As such, this assumption would appear to negate the possibility that it was a planned and/or targeted attack. However, though this may seem like a sensible conclusion, we cannot know this. I believe [and it is just my own opinion] that it can only remain a viable theory if Hanratty *was* part of a wider conspiracy [rather than acting alone] and had some help in accomplishing the abduction – thereafter, however, he would have been on his own.

The timelines are crucial in determining whether Hanratty *could* have been the gunman. From his own testimony he arrived in Liverpool at 3.30 pm. Mrs Dunwoodie placed him at the sweetshop by 4 pm. The pro-Hanratty lobby have strenuously disputed this timing and intimated that it could have been as late as 5.30 pm [incidentally, purported later sightings of Hanratty in Liverpool on the 22nd could also be attributed to his presence there on the 23rd]. This one and half hours is fundamental to the case, as is the minimum time it would have taken to get from Liverpool to Dorney Reach. In assessing this, we must consider what options Hanratty had available to him. From his own testimony the train could take 3 hours and 35 minutes to travel between Euston station in London and Lime Street station in Liverpool. The sweetshop was in Scotland Road (opposite a cinema) to which he took a bus. This was a relatively short distance by bus, so taking into account various small delays between disembarking from the train to reaching the sweetshop [it is not known how long he waited for the bus], Mrs Dunwoodie's time frame is probably not far off. Hanratty's own testimony did not indicate any great delay in this journey, therefore, to assume approximately 4 pm is reasonable. Hanratty had been in search of a Carlton or Tarleton Avenue, neither of which exists – the fact that he did not know where he was going may (again) *suggest* that he was not going to need to rush back to London; however, he may not have been expecting to take all that long to reach the intended address. There is a Carlton Street, which is quite close to Scotland Road, which is probably why he was initially directed there; but intriguingly, there is also a Tarleton Street and this is very close to Lime Street Station – another fact that has been conveniently washed over in the past.

Because Hanratty never told the whole truth about to whom he went to see in Liverpool and apparently got the address confused, we can never know whether it really was Tarleton Street and therefore that he *could* have been given to believe (correctly in this case) that it was close to the station, which might imply that he wasn't intending to hang around. So, the conspiracy theory does still have some modicum of potential substance. In the event though, we know he did not go to Tarleton Street, (at least not directly).

The next question is how long Hanratty spent looking for Carlton/Tarleton Avenue. If the clock was ticking towards a rendezvous at Dorney Reach, then he may have called off his search fairly quickly, especially if he had realised that he was on wild goose chase. But he would still have needed to get back to Lime Street in time to catch a return train that would arrive back at Euston in sufficient time. This is another important area for which scant information appears to have been collated. It doesn't seem that the available train times were explored for the 22nd. Nevertheless, in relation to the 21st August, during cross-examination of Hanratty in a bid to undermine his Liverpool alibi of the 22nd, the prosecution stated that there was a train that left Lime Street at 5.15 pm, arriving at Euston at 9.15 pm. It is not now possible to establish what trains were running on the 22nd, so we can only speculate: it would seem likely that there were trains running at these approximate times on a daily basis; it would also therefore follow that Hanratty could not have intended to return on an a much earlier train. If we assume Hanratty gave up his search soon after leaving the sweetshop in Scotland Road, then hypothetically he could have arrived back at Lime Street in time to catch the late afternoon train. He could even have got a taxi, which would have saved some time. The train journey suggested by the prosecution to have occurred on the 21st would certainly have enabled him to get to the Vienna Hotel by 11 pm; Dorney Reach on the 22nd by 9.45 pm is less credible, verging on the impossible. But we don't know the train times for the 22nd. Given that the train to Liverpool took about 3 hours 35 minutes, then it must be possible that the return train could have arrived before 9 pm; interestingly, the train journey between Liverpool and Euston is still about the same today, while the duration can vary enormously regardless of whether it is peak or off-peak. Disregarding a few extreme exceptions, the variation today is as much as 2 hours. Obviously, applying modern standards to 1961 is somewhat incongruous, what it does demonstrate is that even if modern trains are faster, journey times can be almost doubled on some runs.

There is no necessity to labour on this issue any further: the reasonable conclusion has to be that Hanratty could have made it to Dorney Reach at 9.45 pm on the 22nd [using the train], though it would certainly have helped had he been assisted. The trip between Euston and Dorney Reach would have required a car to have realistically been possible within the time limitations. I don't think it is remotely credible that Hanratty acquired a car himself after arriving at Euston and drove to Dorney Reach. This scenario still requires a conspiracy in order to work.

If we now step back a little in time to when Hanratty was still searching for his Liverpool contact after leaving the sweetshop in Scotland Road, we can imagine that he would be getting increasingly frustrated. Perhaps having conceded that he was not going to locate his contact [they may even have had an approximate meeting time planned] then he would need to decide what to do next. In his original alibi he of course indicated that he stayed in Liverpool, but even assuming there was no urgency for him to return to London, he may still have decided to go back. Only one other realistic option was "available": he either had to hire and/or steal a car.

By all accounts Hanratty was a capable driver and had a wide experience of different vehicles, but he did not have a licence; he had learned to drive by illegal means and most of his experience came from driving stolen vehicles. Though he had no driving convictions (as such), it is not hard to imagine what kind of driver he would have been, i.e. not a considerate one and potentially dangerous. The lack of convictions frankly proves nothing, contrary to his defence and the pro-Hanratty lobby's contention. When Gregsten's Morris Minor was sighted in London on the morning of the 23rd (by at least two witnesses), it was said to have been being driven fast and "erratically"; their presumption was that the driver was inexperienced and therefore could not have been Hanratty. In addition to the witness testimony, when the car was recovered it was found to have sustained damage to both ends, indicating that the driver had been in several different scrapes.

Considering the circumstances, combined with tiredness and stress, would anyone be driving in an exemplary or casual manner? I don't think that this is in the *least* bit surprising.

Since 1961 the British road network has changed immensely, so it is not possible to follow the precise route that Hanratty would have had to. He could have used the old A6 for quite a lot of the journey, but much of this has been upgraded and incorporated into other routes, so it is not possible to trace an exact route today. Using the modern road system, depending upon which of the most direct routes is taken and assuming Scotland Road, Liverpool to Marsh Lane, Dorney Reach, without any deviation, the journey time could vary anything between 3 - 5 hours (abiding by the speed limits). In 1961 the roads were generally much poorer than they are today; conversely, there were lesser speed limits, a great deal less traffic and far less chance of being caught driving badly. On this basis, I would estimate that the journey could have comfortably taken Hanratty around 4 hours. If he had left Liverpool between 4.30 and 5.30 pm, then he could have made it to Dorney Reach before 9.45 pm and conceivably a lot earlier. Yet there is no logical reason as to why he would have taken a route that ended at Dorney Reach. Unless we again assume a conspiracy, then his only tenable reason would be an unintentional one – who hasn't got lost on a long car trip, even when one is vaguely familiar with the route? In those days, road signs and markings were significantly poorer; he could have easily made a wrong turn and perhaps the vehicle broke down or run out of petrol. This being the case, it would of had to been in the general vicinity of Dorney Reach for Hanratty to have made the rest of the way on foot – this scenario, though not generally consistent with a conspiracy, still would not necessarily exclude it.

Whatever the precise reason, if Hanratty arrived at the vicinity of the scene of the abduction predominantly by road, what happened to the car? There are no known police reports in relation to the recovery of stolen vehicles in that area at the time; had there been one for a car originating from Liverpool, we might have a smoking gun (metaphorically speaking). But, we don't. Equally, though, it is not known whether the police made any specific enquiries along these lines, nor was it an issue that got any attention in court. Depending on where exactly the car could have been abandoned, it is feasible that the police overlooked the connection; or, someone unscrupulous recovered the vehicle, failed to report it and the car disappeared into oblivion. It can only be concluded that it was not impossible. One remaining explanation could be that the car broke down some distance from Dorney Reach, but Hanratty managed to thumb a lift relatively quickly; then, perhaps due to tiredness, he realised he wasn't going where he wanted when already well off course and was then dropped off (possibly from the A4) near Dorney Reach. Again, there is nothing to support this theory except that it is possible – witnesses do not *always* come forward.

Fact is often stranger than fiction; mysteries often evolve from mundane origins: where do all those lost socks go? When something is unknown it is a mystery; once solved it often transpires to be pretty obvious.

Continuing with the stolen vehicle theme, if we suppose Hanratty found himself stranded in the Buckinghamshire countryside, what would his next course of action be? Logically, to find some further means to get home. He could have tried thumbing another lift, had no luck, or was on the wrong side of the carriageway and chose not to try crossing it, so decided to wander into the village of Dorney Reach in hope of finding a car to steal. In 1961 there were far less car owners, so finding a suitable vehicle in a small village might have proven to be a challenge. Then he spots a car pulling off the road into a field. By this stage he might have become rather desperate: hijacking a car may have become an attractive option.

Chapter Two

Means and Motivation

Having established that it is hypothetically possible for Hanratty to have committed this crime (albeit circumstantially), the next issue that must be tackled is why it spiralled out of control, transforming from a *relatively* minor one into a capital crime. Given the two cited most reasonable precursory grounds for committing this crime, [i.e. (i) to steal or hijack a vehicle as result of being stranded in the middle of nowhere; (ii) as the hired operative of a conspiracy to frighten Gregsten and Storie into ending their relationship], why did the gunman then magnify the crime into a protracted and excessively serious one?

To answer this it is first necessary to examine Hanratty's psychology to assess whether he had the capacity to commit rape and murder, before considering why it might have happened, assuming (as we are) that the gunman did not initiate the whole episode with that intention.

James Hanratty was born in 1936 and would have been nearly aged 25 in August 1961. He was of humble background, eldest of four brothers. Though born in Kent, his family later moved to London (Wembley). At the age of 11 he was a pupil at *St.James' Catholic High School*, Burnt Oak in the North London borough of Barnet; he ended his education at the age of 15, then attending *Kingsbury Secondary Modern* in the London borough of Brent, taking a job as a 'Refuse Sorter' for Wembley Borough Council. The following year he suffered a serious head injury falling from a bicycle: he was unconscious for 10 hours and was kept in hospital for 9 days. Shortly after this he left the family home (without warning) to find casual work as road haulier in Brighton, Sussex. Eight weeks later he was discovered semi-conscious in the street suffering from hunger and/or exposure. As a result of this, due to a mistaken diagnosis of brain haemorrhage, he underwent a craniotomy. It has since been suggested that he was likely suffering from post-concussion syndrome [PCS] (or possibly had epilepsy). Following this, however, he managed to hold down a steady job for 3 years as a mechanical shovel driver for a company making breeze blocks in Bedford. [Incidentally, his familiarity with the Bedford area might explain why he chose to go in that direction when leaving London during the crime]. But, about a month before his 18th birthday he was up in court in Harrow where he was convicted of stealing a motorcycle; he also had no insurance or driving licence. Soon after this, he got his call-up for National Service, only to fail the medical examination having been found unfit for duty as a result of his illiteracy.

It is around about this time that he became drawn into London's criminal underworld (where he was befriended by one Charles 'Dixie' France,) and soon realised that making money from illicit gambling and various criminal enterprises was a whole lot easier than honest hard graft – it paid better too! Before long his primary sources of income came from house breaking and he was not averse to stealing the odd car when he wanted one. Inevitably he found himself regularly spending time in prison: during the period of October 1955 to March 1960 he spent a total of 58 months inside. On release from Strangeways [24.03.1960] he returned to the family home, but soon disappeared again, going to work for British Steel in Middlesbrough; then after only a week, he was back. This time he was determined to knuckle down and go straight. His father, desperate to reform his son's wayward behaviour, left his job, cashed in his pension and invested it in the necessary materials to enable them to establish their own window cleaning operation. For 3 months Hanratty worked alongside his father; all seemed to be going well, well enough in fact for his parents to leave him in charge of the business while they took a holiday break in Southsea. Hanratty managed to sustain his commitment to his new trade for about 3 days on his own, before the lure of Soho and easy money in London from housebreaking took its toll: they didn't set eyes on him again until he was incarcerated in connection with the "A6 Murder".

Hanratty has always been painted by his supporters as some sort of lovable rogue, an innocuous reprobate, a rough-diamond. It is understandable that his family and friends (for the most part) would prefer to remember him in this way, but it is more difficult to comprehend why so many intelligent people have so readily bought-in to this whitewash. The real truth is that he was a habitual criminal; a blight upon decent hard working society.

He loved money and as a prolific burglar and car thief, he was often flush with wads of cash, which he spent largely on fancy clothes, hotels, gambling, night clubs and women: nothing particularly surprising there, of course, though his interest in women did extend to prostitutes, whom he frequented regularly. He also loved cars: by all accounts he had a wide knowledge of driving them (and stealing them), making him an experienced and supposedly skilful driver, despite never having acquired a licence. He was however convicted for driving with no insurance or licence – though not for any specific *driving* offence.

We can therefore reasonably conclude that Hanratty was an inveterate, recidivistic, low-life crook. In all probability he had an amoral personality. This does not necessarily make him of violent disposition or a sexual deviant; indeed there is absolutely no indication of either. Anecdotal evidence indicates that he was a very likeable person – at least on the surface – quite charming. No doubt this is why everyone who knew him did not imagine him committing this crime and why intelligent people such as Paul Foot, Jean Justice (et al) and Bob Woffinden were genuinely convinced that he was innocent. The problem is though that no one knows what really goes on inside other people's heads; someone with a *Jekyll and Hyde* character may be able to suppress their darker side to the greater extent. One could cite many examples of superficially inoffensive people who have gone on to commit essentially motiveless despicable crimes: John Wayne Gacy, Dennis Rader, Ted Bundy, Peter Sutcliffe, Harold Shipman... The list is endless. I'm not, however, suggesting that Hanratty should be grouped together with this type of offender, only that they poignantly demonstrate that no one can ever know what someone else may be capable of.

Nevertheless, in contrast to Hanratty's outward persona, throughout his troubled life various experts have described him in some very unflattering terms. Though certainly not stupid – he was streetwise, cunning and had plenty of criminal "nouse" – he was of below average intelligence [possibly retarded] and of low intellect. Perhaps, more significantly – according to assessments made by two separate prison doctors, years apart – he was potentially psychopathic. He had also been described as a pathological liar and socially/emotionally immature. In view of these revelations, I really do *not* think it is possible, as his trial defence and the pro-Hanratty lobby would have it, to insist that he was *not* capable of rape or murder. That doesn't *necessarily* mean that he was, either – at least, not under normal circumstances.

There is a further incidental adjunct to assessing Hanratty's capacity for serious criminal behaviour. It is a known fact that serious head injuries can profoundly alter an individual's personality and there are numerous examples of convicted psychopaths having sustained a serious head injury earlier in their life. Moreover, schizophrenia can theoretically affect anyone at any time, irrespective of any prior psychological conditions. Recreational drugs are recognised as potentially causing neurological problems that can lead to schizophrenia and psychosis. Granted that there is no evidence whatsoever that Hanratty ever dabbled in drugs (which were not prevalent at the time, anyway) – in fact he didn't even smoke or drink; neither is this something that has previously ever been suggested – that does not preclude the possibility. Equally, he was never diagnosed to have schizophrenia, but that cannot exclude a schizophrenic episode.

Returning to the two scenarios being presented as the catalysts for the crime, we must now speculatively examine how each situation could have led to the subsequent outcome, principally based on Storie's testimony of the event:

(i) The Vehicle Hijack Scenario: Hanratty approaches the vehicle unaware at this stage that there are two occupants, anticipating a single male driver. As he happened to be carrying a gun [perhaps for protection for his meeting in Liverpool] this was obviously the perfect weapon with which to threaten the driver. When Gregsten winds down the window, Hanratty now realises that there is also a female occupant, which does slightly change the situation. Having had a lengthy walk and experiencing a degree of stress, he initially opts to get into the vehicle to give himself a chance to think. He takes the ignition key, partly because he's going to need it, but also so that the driver cannot throw it into the dark field – he needs to maintain full control of the situation. Unsure what to do and feeling slightly vulnerable with the car parked near the road, he orders Gregsten to drive further into the field to buy some thinking time and enable himself the chance to relax. We can only guess what was going through his mind at this stage. He engaged them in conversation for a time, then made them hand over their money and watches [oddly, he later returned their watches – perhaps he decided they were of no value]. After about 45 minutes, possibly spooked by activity at a cottage adjoining the field – though too distant to be a real threat – Hanratty suddenly announces that he wants to get food and then return to the field. Initially, he intended Gregsten to be put in the boot of the car, but was talked out of this by Storie who convinced him that Gregsten could be asphyxiated. Consequently, he decided that Gregsten could drive. During this episode, Storie noticed that the gunman was covering the bottom half of his face with a cowboy-style handkerchief. Throughout the ordeal, the gunman had constantly insisted that Gregsten and Storie not turn around, so they had few opportunities to see his face; it was also dark.

The fact that Hanratty hid his identity, indicates that there was no intent to kill – at least, not to begin with. So, why didn't he just take the car and go? I would suggest that Valerie Storie's presence is the key to this mystery. At first, Hanratty may have been reluctant to leave a woman stranded in the middle of a field at night, which we can probably put down to 1960's "chivalry". He may then have realised that she was quite attractive and perhaps, not altogether "virtuous". This may seem a little archaic and naive today, but by the superficial moralistic standards of the early 1960's, such an attitude would not have been malapropos. Although there is no evidence of Hanratty being violent toward women, we know he was licentious (particularly for the times) and liked the more wanton type. No disrespect is intended to Valerie Storie, but she would presumably have appealed to Hanratty and he may have started to entertain some amorous thoughts towards her. The idea of putting Gregsten in the car boot may have been a ploy to get Storie alone with him; outright rape may not have been on the agenda at that point, but he may have been pondering some sort of sexual encounter.

It is interesting that there was no earnest effort to obtain food after they left the cornfield [though they did attempt to buy some milk]; neither was there any attempt to return to that location – perhaps because this never was

Hanratty's true intention. Instead, they embarked on a bizarre journey through the outskirts of London, occasionally stopping to get more petrol and once to buy cigarettes. This was all quite risky: in those days, petrol stations had attendants to dispense your petrol; though it did mean that no one need leave the vehicle, it did heighten the chance of witnesses whose suspicions might be raised. Buying cigarettes was particularly strange, as Hanratty wasn't known to smoke, though Storie had the impression that the gunman wasn't a regular smoker – perhaps it was the stress? This all seemed rather aimless. Hanratty was very nervous throughout and clearly demonstrated anxiety about how the car was being driven; Storie described him as a "back-seat driver". When asked if he drove himself, he said he did; many of the comments he made did indicate that he knew how to drive. So, whatever was the point of this little mystery tour – there was clearly no plan?

Continuing the theme that Hanratty was erotically desirous of Storie, I would suggest that he was looking for some prospect of either ditching Gregsten or allowing him to escape, without rousing suspicion of a nefarious purpose. He may also have been desperately trying to think of somewhere to take Storie. Hanratty was perhaps contemplating persuading Storie to have sex, rather than overtly forcing her: psychologically, he could convince himself that it wasn't rape.

Once this predicament had progressed for some time, Hanratty would probably be in a real quandary as to what he should now do, *in general*, and eventually concluded that whatever that was, it would be advantageous to leave behind the heavily populated London suburbs and relocate to somewhere much more secluded. So, they headed out of London, in a Northerly direction. Eventually, they were back into the countryside. Hanratty stated that he was tired and needed "a kip". Whether this was a ruse or true, or possibly both, is unknown, but he was apparently unbothered by Gregsten and Storie whispering to each other, which could indicate weariness. It would not be hard to imagine that he would be getting pretty tired and frustrated by this stage, and keen to bring a close to the proceedings. Finally, he settled on an isolated lay-by off the A6, near Clophill.

What his precise intentions were he never divulged to his captives, but under the premise of needing to sleep, he determined to tie them both up. Not having much success, he noticed a bag in the front footwell, which he ordered to be passed back to him. Gregsten may or may not have been attempting to disarm the gunman, but in any event, Gregsten's actions were perceived as a threat and the gunman fired the gun twice. Whether this was an accident, an unintentional over-reaction, or perhaps just an excuse, we will never know, but Gregsten was dead. This immediately changed everything. An argument subsequently broke out between Storie and the gunman as to whether they should obtain medical help or whether Gregsten was already dead. After 15-20 minutes, the gunman accepted that Gregsten was dead, using some laundry from the bag to cover his face. This would appear to indicate some shame (if not guilt) about what he had done; he was not eager to escape, however. His attention now turned to Storie. It is impossible to know whether he had already decided to kill Storie, or whether rape was always the intention. Storie tried to resist, but she was at the gunpoint of a killer – what choice did she have? There is no impression from the testimony that has been made public that the rape was in any sense violent; Storie, fearing for her life, most likely just acceded. It is also possible, though it has never been previously intimated, that Storie could have offered herself to him in a desperate bid for self-preservation: something she would be unlikely to later admit to, albeit entirely understandable, given the circumstances. In either case, she wouldn't seem to have put up much resistance, which though in no sense excuses the rapist, may have eased his twisted conscience.

Following the rape, the gunman did not appear to be in any rush; he and Storie talked and argued for around 20 minutes, before she was able to convince him to take the car and go. First, Gregsten's body had to be removed, though: the gunman wanted Storie to do this because he wished to avoid getting blood on his clothes, but in the event he did have to assist her. Storie dragged Gregsten's body to the edge of the lay-by then got permission to reclaim some of their belongings. The gunman took a rug from the boot to use as a cover to put over the driver's seat, stating again that he wanted to avoid getting bloodied, also wiping the steering wheel. He then asked Storie to start the car and explain how it worked; she then went and sat on the ground next to Gregsten's body. The gunman now dithered before telling Storie that he would need to knock her out so that she couldn't immediately run for help. She pleaded that she wouldn't and offered him a pound note if he would go quickly; the gunman was slightly baffled by the fact that she had more money, but took it and walked away. However, he shortly turned and fired several shots into her, reloaded, then fired 3 more shots. Storie, having miraculously survived, had the presence of mind to play dead. The gunman kicked her before leaving. He seemed to have no trouble driving the car away at speed.

It should be noted that following the murder of Gregsten, we cannot be certain that Storie's account of events, particularly those leading up to the rape, are completely accurate: from her perspective, she was sexually assaulted against her will, regardless of exactly how that came about. All we can ascertain is the apparent lack of physical violence, which I believe does promote plausibility in the belief that Hanratty was the gunman.

(ii) The Conspiracy Scenario: Hanratty returns from Liverpool (somewhat pushed for time, things not having gone to plan); he then rendezvous with a third party, who most likely is the one [or one of those] whom has engineered the "Gregsten/Storie job". Hanratty would either have been collected from Euston Station or driven to a pre-arranged meeting place, where he would have abandoned his vehicle to be taken to Dorney Reach by the third party; this third party could also have supplied the gun and ammunition, [but this would have had to be sometime prior to the 22nd]. This might explain why no one was seen to be walking along the relevant roads around the time of the kidnap. It can only be presumed that the strategy was to frighten the couple and leave them stranded in the middle of a cornfield. Had he been hired to kill Gregsten and Storie, the psychological turmoil that might have then lead to the following sequence of events is appreciably easier to comprehend, it just doesn't seem particularly credible; but it certainly is not impossible, so perhaps this should not be discounted as the intention from the outset, given that it does make the gunman's behaviour more intelligible, (particularly if the gunman had not previously killed). Nonetheless, assuming that murder was not originally on the agenda, what had then transpired would most likely have followed a similar progression to that described in the first scenario.

The murder weapon is one of the key factors in this case. It was claimed that Hanratty did not have a gun, nor indeed had any obvious reason to want one. The gun was a .38 Enfield revolver, which had been used extensively as a sidearm in WWII. This type of gun would have been relatively abundant in the criminal underworld of the late 1950's and early 1960's. A powerful, though unsophisticated weapon: non-automatic, requiring manual removal of spent cartridge cases. It is certainly a gun that one could associate with the poorer-class of criminal. Why a petty criminal like Hanratty would feel the need to own a gun is anyone's guess: protection, bravado, ego, as sense of empowerment, or perhaps just an unhealthy interest? Unfortunately for Hanratty, several of his close criminal associates apparently provided statements that could be interpreted as meaning that he had sought to obtain a gun (or at least had an interest in doing so) and, according to Louise Anderson, had actually got one.

Donald Slack was a long time friend who had taken bets from him; Hanratty clearly trusted him. Slack purportedly had told DSupt Acott of a conversation which Hanratty subsequently confirmed, along the lines that housebreaking was no longer viable and that in order to go after cash to get rich, a "shooter" was necessary. However, Hanratty was insistent that this was not a serious remark – just talking big. Strangely, it transpired that Acott had been bluffing, Slack having made a statement completely in contradiction of the claim; it is therefore, difficult to conclude anything substantive from this, though it is interesting that Hanratty didn't simply deny it. Charles France, Hanratty's long standing friend and criminal associate, told Acott that Hanratty had spoken about disposing of unwanted stolen items under the back seat of a bus: this was very damaging, because the murder weapon had been placed under the back seat of the 36A bus, in just the way described.

Louise Anderson was another close friend and criminal associate of Hanratty. Anderson was a prolific handler of stolen goods. She and Hanratty had regular "business" dealings – she was in fact his primary 'fence'. Louise was also a friend with whom he often stayed (at her flat), though there was never any romantic relationship. At the pre-trial magistrates hearing, she came into contact with Charlotte France (wife of Charles France); both were giving evidence, along with Charlotte's daughter Carole France. They had never met before and were unaware of their connection. Charlotte reported that she had been upset by a conversation with Anderson whereby she was told that she knew that Hanratty had a gun and that he kept it at "Dixie's" place in a carrier bag in a cupboard among some blankets. Charlotte was shocked, as Anderson's account certainly seemed to confirm that Hanratty had been hiding a gun in *her* home.

It is important to note that Anderson never gave this evidence in court or made any formal statement to such effect. Carole France later made a statement recalling how this event had unnerved her just prior to being required to give evidence. It is the pro-Hanratty lobby's allegation that Anderson and the Frances were intimidated by the police into giving evidence against Hanratty, on the basis that they were pliable given their own criminal complicities – which were uncovered during the police investigation of Hanratty; moreover, Hanratty was probably considered to be responsible (albeit unwittingly) for incriminating them. The fact is that no one knows whether either the Frances or Anderson would have been willing to give misleading or fraudulent evidence against Hanratty. Though it cannot be completely disregarded, there are some flaws to this hypothesis. For example, the idea that Anderson (under the direction of the police) invented the gun story in order to unsettle Charlotte and Carole France prior to the magistrates' hearing does seem somewhat preposterous. Despite there being far more damaging things that could have been invented, why did Anderson not give this evidence at the trial? This would have been extremely damning. And as highlighted earlier, why would the Frances give evidence supporting Hanratty's presence in London on the 21st which then supported his alibi that he was in Liverpool on the 22nd, when the prosecution case asserted that the alibi for the 22nd had been "faked" on the 21st, thereby contradicting that particular line of evidence?

There has never been any admission by anyone during the fifty odd years since the crime was committed that substantiates that any coercion of witnesses occurred or that any evidence was invented, distorted or withheld that would have had any bearing on the outcome of the trial – with one probable exception [to be dealt with later] which was made evident at the trial and related to a statement allegedly provided by a witness at the scene of crime. Louise Anderson made a number of damaging claims against Hanratty, which on the face of it could be construed as being disingenuous, as they were known to be close friends. Though there was no implication that she ever felt personally threatened, she did state that Hanratty had on occasion been known to make salacious remarks: this isn't especially incriminating, but it certainly undermined Hanratty's character in a very unhelpful way. The inconvenient truth is though, all of the evidence given by Hanratty's friends and associates at the trial were relatively innocuous, albeit occasionally unhelpful to his cause. Had these witnesses been pressurized by the prosecution into giving false evidence, surely they could have manufactured something far more damaging. The fact that Anderson did not recount the gun story in court, suggests that though she (and likewise, others) had been compelled to give evidence against their former friend, there remained a reluctance to do so, which would very easily explain the considerable stress that Anderson (and the Frances) exhibited during the court appearances; it did have all the hallmarks of melodramatic performance, but was in fact entirely genuine and spontaneous, brought on by a combination of friendship, criminal allegiances and an element of denial confused with the terrible realisation that they had been intimately collaborating with a rapist/murderer; possibly even acting as inadvertent accomplices.

Much has been made of Charles France's suicide, which occurred soon after Hanratty's execution. The pro-Hanratty lobby have tirelessly attempted to imply that this was because of guilt on the part of France, yet this supposition is pure wishful thinking. There is not a shred of evidence to support such an assertion; in fact, what evidence there is, points entirely to the contrary. There is little likelihood that the exact reasons for France's suicide will ever be known (or disclosed), but everyone would agree that Hanratty's guilt (whether real or apparent) was a major contribution in exacerbating his depressive state, if not the actual cause of it. I don't believe this is in the least bit surprising, given the close association that Hanratty had with Charles and his family – it is known that Hanratty had even dated Carole.

Another key factor that has received significant focus in establishing Hanratty's innocence was the gunman's use of gloves. It is a known fact that Hanratty's modus operandi as a burglar was not to ever wear gloves. He preferred to carry a handkerchief which he used to wipe anything that he touched and there is no doubt that he was still pursing this tactic in the early August of 1961. It is somewhat ironic that it now would appear that a handkerchief was his evidential undoing. However, the gloves do present a problem as far as identifying Hanratty as the gunman. Anderson gave evidence that she had lost a pair of gloves sometime close to the time of the crime, a detail that did not help Hanratty's case. In truth, this is a probable red herring, as it is doubtful they would have fitted Hanratty. If we consider the conspiracy scenario, then the idea that he would have chosen to use (or been supplied with) gloves for that particular job is perfectly reasonable. The use of gloves in the other scenario is more difficult to reconcile: it is possible that he had recently taken to wearing gloves, which like the handkerchief, he had chosen to carry at all times – perhaps he was trying to be an altogether more sophisticated criminal; or, perhaps they were driving gloves obtained from the stolen vehicle, which he had happened to continue wearing after ditching the car. This is one of those minor details that could be a critical detail, depending on which side of the argument one stands, and one for which there isn't going to be a definitive answer.

Chapter Three

The Principal Evidence

To begin examination of the principal evidence against Hanratty, I would like to start at the end, i.e. with the DNA evidence. This of course was not available until 2001; during the 40 preceding years there was only a tenuous case against Hanratty and that had more holes than a Swiss cheese. The original evidence has to be cherry picked in order to make even a frangible case, whether for or against Hanratty. There was ultimately, a vast collection of witness evidence, but as I have previously established, such testimony is fraught with uncertainty; add to this the mass of contradictory material, the assemblage of dubious characters, poor and incomplete police investigations, disreputable behaviour on the part of the prosecution and ineptness of the part of the defence, and what you have is a recipe to induce severe indigestion. In attempt to circumvent this, I have focused predominantly on the critical aspects of the evidence and avoided much of the extraneous minutiae – of which there is considerable volumes – and anything that is overly equivocal or potentially meretricious. Lamentably, this doesn't actually leave a great deal.

DNA profiling is a highly specialised scientific discipline, which has developed enormously since the original technique was reported in 1986. It relies heavily upon a process known as Polymerase Chain Reaction [PCR] to amplify genetic material by DNA replication, to produce samples in viable quantities to be accurately analysed. The method uses STR's [Short Tandem Repeats] that occur in regions of the DNA that are subject to considerable variation between individuals. CODIS [the FBI's Combined DNA Index System] uses 13 loci, i.e. 13 specific DNA genomic locations; each location theoretically gives rise to something of the order of 10 possible variations, therefore, there is roughly a 1 in 10 chance of each loci matching between two random individuals, such that for each loci that match there is a 10-fold increase in improbability. So, if 13 loci can be matched, the chances of that is 10 multiplied 13 times, or 1 in 10000000000000 [i.e. 10,000 billion]. In fact, it could be as much as 1 in a quintillion. The UK uses the SGM+ 11 system, which matches 11 loci; this is compatible with National DNA Database which uses 10 loci. It is in effect a statistical tool and does not involve matching the entire genome, (much of which is identical between all individuals, anyway). Sample quality can affect the results, because it may result in some loci matches being inconclusive and obviously the fewer loci that can be definitively matched, the lower the probability that the samples are from the same individual. This is a critical factor in DNA profiling. In the Hanratty case, the details of the DNA analysis are not readily available, but given the attitude of the Court of Appeal and Hanratty's 2002 defence team in respect to it, we must presume that there was a high statistical probability in the matching against Hanratty's DNA – the defence team conceded that if contamination could be excluded, then Hanratty *must* be guilty.

The DNA Evidence

A sample of Storie's underwear (containing preserved semen) was found in 1991 and the handkerchief used to wrap the murder weapon (containing preserved mucous) was located in the archives of Berkshire police in 1997. It is unfortunate that some original physical evidence was destroyed over the years and it is known that a broken vial was amongst the surviving evidence, giving rise to the claim of contamination. It is reasonable to assume that historically, none of this evidence was handled in a particularly clinically rigorous manner, nor would have been stored in perfect conditions. However, subsequent to their later discovery, there is no reason to presume that they were not thereafter handled in scientifically proper manner. Unfortunately, neither the precise circumstances surrounding the reclamation of these samples, nor their relative condition at that time, is completely clear. We therefore, must trust that the samples were found to be analytically viable in respect to the criteria of good practice required by the DNA sequencing laboratory; the comparison sample DNA was extracted from Hanratty's exhumed corpse. In addressing any ambivalence one might accord to this evidence it is worth noting that Hanratty's relatives were formerly convinced that the DNA analysis would exonerate Hanratty; only when the results did not support their position did they seek to discredit that evidence. The 2002 Court of Appeal concluded that there was no justification to suppose that the samples tested had been contaminated and took the view that the "DNA evidence, standing alone, is certain proof of guilt". While I believe that is not completely beyond debate, such a judgement is extremely persuasive, given that the judges had all of the facts at their disposal, combined with their considerable knowledge and experience. Had they reached a converse denouement, I sincerely doubt that anyone would be making much of a complaint.

So, presuming efficacy of the analytical process and the sufficient integrity of the samples, what does the DNA evidence actually prove? For the purposes of this evaluation, the two samples must be considered in isolation. The underwear sample is the most controversial, because the analysis identified two male DNA profiles: Hanratty's and an unknown. Frustratingly, the unknown has been assumed to belong to Gregsten and (to my knowledge) no attempt has ever been made to prove this. If it were shown to be Gregsten's, given that these were the only profiles found (other than Storie's), ignoring any potential contamination, this would be definitive proof. But unless the second profile is identified, one must consider that this sample could have been contaminated and, worse still, that the unknown DNA belongs to the "real" killer. Therefore, it is probably better to disregard this evidence, except as essentially supporting the handkerchief result. With the handkerchief, however, no other DNA was identified – only Hanratty's. I think it is inconceivable that this evidence would not have been mishandled [at least to begin with] at the time of the case, simply because the contamination issue would not have been realised, while the handkerchief itself could not have yielded anything of use to the police at that time. Interestingly, it is worth noting that the handkerchief was never unequivocally identified as belonging to Hanratty until the DNA analysis; prior to that, it was simply assumed probable on the basis that he was found guilty. He was known to carry a handkerchief at all times, by his own admission, but so did the vast majority of men in 1961. Nothing relating to the handkerchief was specifically associated with Hanratty, until the mucous was analysed in 1999 & 2001. So, why is this so damning?

The fact that only Hanratty's DNA was detected in the mucous sample effectively denies the possibility that the mucous itself had been contaminated. In order to sustain the contamination argument, one is expected to accept that the DNA of the individual who deposited the mucous had completely degraded away, while Hanratty's DNA had fully survived despite having got there by transfer and that the originators DNA would have been in greater abundance within the sample; it also requires a belief that while Hanratty's DNA had contaminated this sample, no one else's did or if it had, that it also completely degraded away. It may not be an impossible claim, but common sense would suggest that the likelihood of such an occurrence is so utterly negligible as to be not worthy of consideration. One may just as well propose that the gunman was an alien.

In conclusion, if one accepts the veracity of the DNA profiling evidence in relation to the handkerchief, then we know that the murder weapon was wrapped in a handkerchief used by Hanratty. As the gun was found on the 36A bus the evening of the day of the murder, it would be highly implausible to imagine that anyone other than Hanratty had concealed it in the *used* handkerchief, particularly given the restricted time interval. Whether or not he had then placed it on the bus, or whether some accomplice did it for him, can only be a matter of conjecture. Exactly when the gun could have been placed there on the 23rd August is still hotly disputed; no one witnessed Hanratty on that bus, nor was anyone else seen acting suspiciously. However, that is just one of those little mysteries that have always clouded this case; in truth, in light of the DNA evidence, this issue is somewhat redundant. The natural logical conclusion must be that Hanratty was the gunman – to concoct any other scenario would require suspending one's disbelief; at the very least, it proves that he was in London on the 23rd, contrary to his infamous Rhyl alibi, which *immediately* makes any case against him much stronger. The pro-Hanratty lobby have tried to make something from the fact that Hanratty willingly volunteered forensic samples, but in 1961 biological evidence was of very limited value; he would most likely not consider there was much risk attached to this and it made him *seem* co-operative.

In the Appendix I have outlined a calculation of the estimated probability that someone else could have had the same DNA profile as Hanratty, such that despite the DNA evidence, the guilty party could still have been somebody else. That probability is 1 in 10 billion. [The reported probability was a 1 in **2.5 million** chance of Hanratty's innocence – which may indicate less than 10 verifiable matched loci, possibly as a result of sample degradation. For comparison, the total number of potential suspects that I estimated in the Appendix was **2.05 million**, and that's a likely over-estimate].

The Cartridge Cases

The Vienna Hotel in Maida Vale was to play a pivotal role in the 'A6 Murder' case. The police were first drawn to this location to investigate a potential suspect – but not Hanratty. The lead had begun at the Alexandra Court Hotel, Finsbury Park (N. London), where a number of guests had observed some strange behaviour on the part of another guest, whom had remained locked in his room since the murder; he had also apparently been pacing up and down. His description bore close resemblance to that reported for the gunman; he was registered as Frederick Durrant. The hotel manager alerted the police on the morning of the 27th August. A routine check quickly proved that the name and address the guest had given were false. They eventually located Durrant in the early evening, when he had returned to the hotel after being out most of the day. Durrant persisted with his false details, so he was taken to the local police station for further questioning. It soon emerged that Durrant was in fact one Peter Louis Alphon of Streatham – this was a name that would become as synonymous with the "A6 murder" case as James Hanratty itself.

Following questioning of Alphon, he was released while further enquiries were conducted and he was told to return to the station the next day. His eventual account of his movements during the critical period placed him at the Vienna Hotel on the night of 22nd August, having arrived there at approx. 11 pm; he had stayed in Room 6, leaving the next morning at approx. 11.45 am. He had gone to the Alexandra Court Hotel at approx. 5 pm on the 23rd August.

The next major development in the case occurred on the 11th September: the Vienna Hotel was owned by an Austrian, Frederick Pichler – he also owned another hotel. The overall manager employed at the Vienna in August & September of 1961 was Robert Crocker – it was a short-lived appointment. The hotel was run by a staff of four: Spaniards Juliana Galves and her husband, plus another couple, Florence Snell and William Glickberg. Glickberg was however an alias for a rather unsavoury character better known as William Nudds. Together, Snell and Nudds were by all accounts a dishonest waste of space. They had been "working" at the hotel for a month when Crocker was called-in to investigate a theft of £5 (which is the equivalent of ca £100 in 2014). Crocker quickly concluded who the culprits were and being aware of their general lackadaisical attitude, he sacked them with immediate effect. Despite Nudds abusive reaction, Crocker was persuaded to allow the couple to stay in the hotel one more night and gave them a week's wages in lieu of notice. It never was established who had actually employed them in the first place – Crocker assumed it must have been Pichler. Following his debacle with Nudds and Snell, Crocker decided to inspect all the rooms, with Juliana Galves assisting. Upon entering Room 24 [a large room containing a double bed and 3 singles, which was effectively at basement level] Crocker examined an upholstered chair that appeared to be damaged; upon doing so, something fell on the floor: it was a .38 cartridge case. Galves discovered another on top of the chair. Crocker was vaguely aware that the police had enquired about one of the guests on the 27th August, so he notified them of his finding. Somewhat incredibly, with the war only having ended 16 years before it wouldn't necessarily have been regarded as odd to find spent bullet cases and had there not already been police interest in the hotel, it might not have been reported – one of the many ironic and coincidental events that surrounds this case.

The cartridge cases were examined at the Metropolitan Police forensic lab and were positively identified as having come from the gun used in the "A6 Murder". Crocker made a statement to the effect that Alphon had been booked into the hotel for the night of the 22nd August and that the cartridge cases may have been connected to him. However, Alphon had been in Room 6 and according to Galves had arrived at about 11.30 pm – so therefore, could not have been the gunman. On the 13th September, Galves revised her statement, admitting that she had not seen Alphon arrive and only observed him shortly before he left the hotel. The room had actually been booked by phone on the morning of the 22nd. As a result of this revelation, Alphon had no alibi for the period of the abduction: he was now the number one suspect; but there was a problem, because Alphon had not stayed in Room 24. Furthermore, Galves' revised statement said that Room 24 had not been occupied since the 16th August. Consequently, further investigations were made into the various guests staying there during the pertinent period; this did not provide any useful leads until closer scrutiny of the hotel books revealed that on the night of the 21st August Room 24 had been occupied by a 'J. Ryan'. The police still had

Alphon in the frame, but the presence of this unknown 'J. Ryan' confused the matter.

Enter stage left, William Nudds, an inveterate liar and no-good lowlife layabout. Nudds made a statement on the 15th September indicating that J. Ryan had been allocated Room 24 when he registered on the 21st August. He recalled that he had been brought over from the Broadway Hotel by their staff, arriving between 9 and 11 pm. He had showed him to the room, where Ryan had chosen the single bed on the left, just inside the door. Ryan left the hotel the next morning at around 8.30 am, but returned after a few minutes asking if he could recover something from the room – he was allowed to do this alone. Ryan had then enquired how he could get to Queensway; Nudds told him to walk to Harrow Road, where he could catch a No. 36 bus. Nudds then went on to describe how he had witnessed that Alphon had arrived on the 22nd August at about 11.45 pm and was dealt with by Snell. Snell's statement supported this version of events.

William Nudds had a criminal record as long as his proverbial arm and used a string of different aliases. He was well known to the police and prison authorities as an informer; Florence Snell's reputation wasn't much better: this unfortunately castes considerable doubt over anything that they said about anything; they were certainly open to manipulation – something which the pro-Hanratty lobby have used to advance their case, implying that the Nudds/Snell evidence against Hanratty (i.e.

Ryan) was fabricated. Yet, at the time when Nudds/Snell made these statements, J. Ryan was still a mystery man and the police were focusing their investigation upon Alphon. Indeed, Peter Alphon did seem to make a likely suspect; he is also probably the greatest *red herring* of all time. [His involvement in this case lasted 40 years, until the DNA implicated Hanratty – that involvement is examined in the next chapter.]

Alphon was more firmly implicated when Nudds made a second statement, in which he withdrew his affirmations of the 15th September, after apparently realising that he was originally mistaken and could now offer a definitive account in regards to Alphon at the Vienna Hotel, to wit: Alphon arrived at the hotel at 1 pm on the 22nd August to book a single room, but none were available; nonetheless, Room 24 was offered on the proviso that he might have to share the room if other guests arrived and the price was about double that for a single room. Alphon agreed that he would take the room if no single rooms became available and left his suitcase on the armchair of Room 24; he was allocated a key to the room having paid the cost of a single room, which was recorded as a deposit. On leaving the hotel reception desk, Alphon went to Room 24, but returned soon after and leaving in a hurry, informed Nudds that he would be back very late.

Later that evening, Room 6 became free, following a cancellation. When Alphon had not returned by 2 am, Nudds and Snell decided to go to bed; they left a note for Alphon at Reception (along with the key) to the effect that Room 6 was now available. In the morning, only one guest [Alphon] had not shown for breakfast by 9.50 am, so Nudds went to Room 6: getting no response to his knocking, he let himself in using the pass-key. Alphon was getting dressed; he looked dishevelled and unkempt. When Nudds asked what time he got in, Alphon replied "Eleven o'clock"; he didn't want any breakfast. By 11.45 am, Alphon had still not vacated, but Nudds believed that he must have left soon after that. Nudds went on to clarify that Ryan [Hanratty] had vacated Room 24 at 8.30 am on the 22nd August. His descriptions of the two left no doubt that there were distinct differences and therefore, could be no confusion; Alphon was also portrayed as behaving in an agitated manner, while Ryan [Hanratty] was said to be cool, calm and collected. Snell also made a statement much to the same effect as Nudds'.

Peter Alphon was now strongly ensconced as the prime suspect. On the 22nd September, Alphon was named as being wanted in connection with the "A6 murder" at a press conference. Eight hours later, Alphon surrendered himself to the police at the Cannon Row station. Interviewing began in the early hours of 23rd September and by the afternoon Alphon was appearing in identity parades. Several supposed witnesses of the car either failed to identify anyone or picked someone else; Florence Snell also managed to make an incorrect identification, while Nudds picked out two, one of which *was* Alphon. One other witness (*the only one*) did identify Alphon correctly, but his evidence pertained to an incident 3 days after the murder. However, this was all a precursor to the main event on the 24th September: a parade had been arranged at Guy's Hospital, where Valerie Storie was wheeled out. She also could not identify Alphon, but instead picked out an innocent volunteer. That somewhat put the last nail in the coffin of the case against Alphon.

DSupt Acott re-interviewed Juliana Galves, but she still had nothing of use to add, so he now turned back to Snell and Nudds. By the end of the 25th September, Nudds and Snell had withdrawn their second statements, reaffirming their original accounts. Suddenly it was J. Ryan that was firmly in the frame – but they still didn't know who he was.

The evidence relating to the Vienna Hotel given by Nudds and Snell has been perpetually discredited by the pro-Hanratty camp on the basis that they were untrustworthy and susceptible to police collaboration: the fact that they changed their evidence was apparent proof of this. However, this is a paradoxical assessment of the Nudds/Snell involvement, because it was the second statement they made – undermining their original testimony – which is the most suspect. When they made their original statement there was no reason for them to have lied, nor to implicate anyone – at that point, their accounts didn't incriminate Hanratty [because no one knew Ryan *was* Hanratty] and gave Alphon a solid alibi. Only when Alphon became the police's favourite suspect, did they change their recollections in support of Alphon's supposed culpability. Though there is no proof of any complicity between Nudds/Snell and the police – not then, nor ever since – if there is any suspicion about their part in the whole affair, then it has to be that they probably colluded to strengthen the case against Alphon. When it was realised that Alphon wasn't their man and that this 'J. Ryan' was a better suspect, they were encouraged to return to their original account, as this was conducive in pursuing a case against the mysterious 'J. Ryan', who had then become the police's only real suspect.

The next stage of the enquiry was equally controversial, at least from the pro-Hanratty quarter's perspective. There is still some uncertainty as to exactly how the police made the connection between 'J. Ryan' and James Hanratty. On 26th September they visited the address given by J. Ryan when he booked into the Vienna Hotel; it turned out to be false, but the real owner did have some information of value: he had recently received a letter addressed to 'Mr Ryan'. On opening this letter, Acott found that it had been sent by a car-hire firm in Dublin, Ireland – which was, coincidentally, called Ryan's. Later that afternoon, Acott (and another officer) paid a visit to Hanratty's parents' home. But how did they know Ryan was Hanratty? There never was a clear answer to this, but at the trial it was revealed that the police had tentatively identified Ryan as Hanratty on the 25th September – they did not however reveal their source. This little mystery has been grasped by the pro-Hanratty lobby as indicative of some sort of conspiracy against Hanratty. It may well be that one of Hanratty's criminal associates or a police "grass" put them onto Hanratty; the precise details do appear to have been suppressed, but the fact is that Hanratty *was* Ryan, and there is no dispute in that regard. How the police discovered this is perhaps an infuriating unknown, but ultimately it is irrelevant.

On the 29th September, Hanratty is identified by the Police as the new "A6 Murder" suspect. Hanratty does not seem to have learned of this until the 5th October, at which point he contacted Charles France by telephone, who advised him to turn himself in. But Hanratty decided to phone Acott, instead, protesting his innocence. He called Acott twice more over the next few days, before finally being arrested in Blackpool on the 11th October 1961.

Description of the Gunman

There were a number of witnesses who believed they had seen the gunman – the only meaningful ones related to sightings of the Morris Minor on the morning of the 23rd August. Even those that had genuine credibility were fleeting glimpses, through the moving car's windows. Moreover, at the time they witnesses the vehicle, they would not have consciously thought to make a detailed note of the driver's appearance. Nonetheless, two of the four witnesses did manage to pick out Hanratty, though this may not have been very meaningful because Hanratty was wearing a dark suit and all the others in the parade were in light coloured clothing. The press had recorded that he had been wearing a blue suit when arrested and of course, the gunman's description, along with identikit pictures, had been in the public domain for weeks. Given that the identikit images were a reasonable match to Hanratty – as well as many other people, including Alphon – these identifications don't have much integrity.

The only remotely valid witness was Valerie Storie. Unfortunately, even she didn't have a very clear view of the gunman's face: throughout, he had worn a handkerchief over is nose and mouth; she had few opportunities to properly look at him, and it was dark. But there was at least one occasion when she must have had a full view of his features, even if the light would have been poor, because (by her own testimony) he had forced her to kiss him.

On the 25th September, (the day after the first identity parade,) a second parade was organised at Stoke Mandeville Hospital in Buckinghamshire for Valerie Storie. While she was wheeled up and down the line of 13 men, they were instructed to say "Be quiet, will you, I am thinking" which the gunman had uttered in response to Storie's verbal assault following the shooting of Gregsten. The gunman had had a cockney accent, as did Hanratty – the rest of the parade was made up of volunteers from RAF stations. Hanratty may also have stood out, because he had chosen to wear clothes that were supplied by the police, which were probably ill-fitting and somewhat mismatched, besides being distinctly different to the volunteers' apparel. After 15 to 20 minutes of deliberation, Storie eventually made her choice – it was Hanratty. A dubious identification, perhaps – *albeit the least so* – but an extremely damning one.

The description of the gunman is another controversial issue in this case and one which the Hanratty supporters have regularly latched on to; this was partly due to a piece of police incompetence that subsequently cast suspicion over the accuracy of one element of Storie's original description. John Kerr was the first person to speak to Storie following her discovery at Deadman's Hill. He had been conducting a traffic survey nearby – a two-week holiday job, prior to attending college at Oxford. Though he hadn't witnessed anything himself, he was the first person to take a "statement" from Storie, which he recorded on the back of one of the forms he was using at the time. He subsequently gave this piece of paper to a senior police officer at the crime scene – it was never seen again. This was an embarrassing matter during the trial, because it constituted critical evidence taken soon after the crime was committed and it had disappeared. Or had it? During the trial, when Kerr was called to give his evidence, the form suddenly materialised as

Exhibit 104. Trouble was that Kerr was adamant this was not the form he had used, it was not his writing and it was not what he had written. Nothing ever came of this, but it would seem obvious that this Exhibit had been fraudulently generated. However, I would suggest that the primary reason this was done was to cover-up an unbelievable piece of police ineptitude, possibly by a senior officer. Ultimately, though, it isn't really of much importance. Certainly Kerr was convinced that Storie had told him the gunman had "light fairish hair", which contradicts her official descriptions that he had "brown hair" or "dark brown hair". The fact that Storie was just as adamant that she had never described the gunman's hair as being light-coloured seems to have been less significant to the pro-Hanratty lobby than Kerr's conviction. Whether Storie had initially said this or not really is irrelevant, anyway, because what she said thereafter was consistent. Furthermore, Kerr initially had got the impression that Storie's name was 'Mary', so perhaps he wasn't quite the perfect witness some have made him out to be; and one early press release described the gunman as having *brown* eyes, a probable confusion with the name the gunman had given of (Jim) Brown, both of which go to show how easily misunderstandings can occur.

Storie's description of the gunman was essentially: 5ft 6in, dark brown hair, age 25-30, with large saucer-shaped icy blue-eyes and cockney accent. At the time of the crime, Hanratty was known to have had his naturally reddish hair dyed black. In those days, dyes tended to wash out faster than they grew out, so Hanratty's hair could have been a variety of possible shades; it was never possible to definitively establish its precise shade at the time. Given that it was dark, Hanratty's hair may well have appeared to be brown and either dark or light, depending on how much peripheral light was available to view it, regardless of its exact actual colour. He certainly had blue eyes, (which sometimes could be unnervingly staring,) he was about 5ft 6in, aged 25 and did have a cockney accent. Some mileage has also been made out of what colour suit he was wearing, but frankly, this not especially meaningful one way or the other.

Two identikit images were quickly released, one being the product of witnesses of the Morris Minor. There has always been some confusion over which one was Storie's, but they were generally similar, (although clearly different). The fact is, though, Valerie Storie is the only one who had even a half-decent sense of what the gunman looked like and she has always been unshakeable in her identification of Hanratty.

Incredibly, this is essentially the sum total of the evidence against Hanratty, combined with the supposed circumstantial evidence – that proved only that he *could* have done it – and some suspicious hearsay. Without the DNA, there really is no substantive case against him and there is no question that he should have been acquitted. However, once we combine these snippets of evidence with the DNA, suddenly everything falls into place. Though we still do not have a perfect picture of what happened, the finger of guilt points firmly at Hanratty: the chances that he was innocent are infinitesimal.

Chapter Four

Other Suspect(s)

Peter Alphon is forever synonymous with the "A6 Murder". But did he really have any involvement whatsoever, other than (by pure coincidence) having stayed at the same hotel as Hanratty had the night before the murder, but on the night of the murder, and then becoming a potential suspect due to his strangeness? The case is littered with coincidences: Alphon is *probably* just one of those, i.e. the fact that his catching the police's attention effectively led them to Hanratty, is just one of those bizarre case breakers that aren't *really* that uncommon. Nonetheless, though the DNA apparently exonerates Alphon as the murderer/rapist, is it possible that he was somehow involved in a conspiracy scenario-type roll? But before wandering down this dark secluded road, let's examine what was known about Alphon between 1961 and 1971; why he was ever a suspect in the first place, and indeed, whether there were ever any other suspects.

There does appear to have been one or two alternative ripples in the investigative pool, but nothing is known about these other than the content of the scant press reports. What is indisputable is that there were only ever two serious suspects and once Hanratty was in the frame, the investigation was all but over. Alphon was the first known suspect in the case and initially seemed to tick all the boxes. However, though he was something of a weirdo, there was no more reason to imagine he would kill or rape than there was for Hanratty. He did broadly fit the description and was a rough match with the identikit, but then – so I imagine – were a lot of others. The fact that he had brown eyes and was about 5ft 9in doesn't seem to have ever posed a problem for either the police (at the time), or the pro-Hanratty lobby (ever since) who have found every excuse under the sun to explain away these discrepancies. The reality is that there was never any more "evidence" against Alphon than there was against Hanratty – in fact, somewhat less, which therefore is practically nothing. One side note is that Storie allegedly did admit (following the identity parade with Alphon) that he did look a bit like the gunman – but the fact remains that she did not pick him. What did raise suspicions against Alphon was that he was known to have frequented the pub that Gregsten/Storie used regularly and on the night of the murder, which was not all that far from Dorney Reach. Also, witnesses claimed to have seen a man fitting Alphon's description in that pub that night and, in the general area in the run up to the fateful night.

The most serious issue for Alphon, though, was a possibly connected crime that had occurred in Putney [SW London] in Upper Richmond Road at 1.30 pm on the 7th

September: a Mrs Dalal – a Swedish housewife, who let some of the rooms in her large house – had a visit from an interested party; shortly after she started showing him around one of the rooms for let, he suddenly struck her in the side of the head with something hard, causing her to collapse on the floor. The assailant then placed her face-down on the bed and tied her wrists behind her back with some flex (which he had brought with him). While doing this he told her that he was the "A6 Murderer" and wanted some money – she pretended to be unconscious. He then hit her twice more about the head, gagged her with a silk scarf and bound her ankles with a ribbon. He then proceeded to wipe blood from the back of her head with a pillow, before turning her over onto her back; he then lifted her skirts, at which point Mrs Dalal began to struggle and freeing her hands, managed to evade another blow to the head; she then got the scarf out of her mouth and screamed. After a short scuffle, she escaped to another room, where she opened a window and let out a blood curdling scream. The intruder made haste and left, was nearly caught by some GPO engineers, but successfully extricated himself from the situation, disappearing into Mortlake. The police did yield some evidence: an unknown fingerprint and a photofit. Meanwhile, the "A6 Murder" team were preoccupied with other matters; it was their view that this individual was probably just posing as the "A6 Murderer" to scare the victim. There did not appear to have been any attempt by this man to touch Mrs Dalal under her clothing, so his exact motives remain a mystery.

On the 23rd of September, following his appearance in an identity parade for the "A6 Murderer" (where he had not been picked out), he was placed on second parade, this time for the benefit of Mrs Dalal. Had this have happened if he had not already been associated with the "A6 Murder" is something we shall never know, but amazingly, Mrs Dalal identified him as *her* attacker. He subsequently appeared in another parade, where two men positively identified him as a man they had seen in the City at the time of Mrs Dalal's attack, supporting an alibi that Alphon had supplied on the day he was charged with the Dalal attack. Surprisingly, the case still went to court, though it was a fruitless pursuit: after being granted bail, he returned to court on the 3rd October, whereupon the prosecution requested his discharge; he was awarded costs. However, despite there clearly being no evidence other than the disputed identification, the pro-Hanratty lobby has tended to continue to imply his association with it, when it should just have a veil drawn over it – though no one else was ever charged over the incident.

Peter Louis Alphon was born in 1930, the only child of a French emigrant, Felix Alphonse [the 'se' was dropped when he came to Britain] and Dorset born Gladys Ives. Alphon had been a shy and quiet boy, a loner. He was studious – with a fascination of theology, theosophy and astrology – gaining a scholarship to a London public school. During the war he was evacuated to Horsham (West Sussex), where he stayed with the Durrant family – whose name he later used as an alias. This was an unhappy arrangement: after a few weeks, he requested to be moved elsewhere and he was placed with Theresa Jeal (also in Horsham). According to Mrs Jeal, Alphon was a well-spoken, polite boy, albeit a little nervy; always well-behaved. Others were less complimentary, describing him as a misfit, a friendless attention seeker who was always in trouble. As an adult he existed on the fringes of society, with no occupation; he drifted around, living off his mother. He was also something of a petty criminal and thoroughly disreputable. In Bob Woffinden's book he is described at one point as being a 'hardened criminal', but this borders on the preposterous; if anyone was a 'hardened criminal' it was Hanratty. Nonetheless, there is no doubt that he was a dubious character and something of a social outcast; most people found him to be a bit peculiar. Whether that made him inclined towards murder and rape is an unanswerable question; I would suggest, no more than Hanratty. There is no evidence that he ever committed any serious crime either before or after 1961, so to label him as a deviant is presumptive, though he definitely suffered from personality defects. What is apparent is that he could be pretty unlikeable, which makes him the perfect fall-guy. However, he hardly did himself any favours by subsequently implicating himself as the "A6 Murderer", a performance he maintained (on and off) until 1971, when he finally asserted his innocence resolutely.

What motivated Alphon to embroil himself into the "A6 Murder" controversy will only ever be truly known to him. He certainly delighted in the notoriety it brought him, no doubt revelling in the attention of the media circus. He was never in any danger of being prosecuted for the crime, because by the time he stuck his head above the parapet, Hanratty was already awaiting execution, having lost his chance to appeal. So, Alphon could enjoy the infamy, safe in the knowledge that nothing would ever come of it. The police had decisively eliminated *him* as the gunman.

Accepting his twisted attraction to the case, exacerbated by his own initial involvement as a suspect, there may have been another (possibly, more understandable) motive, that being the greatest temptress of them all: money. This is where another character synonymous with the "A6 Murder" case enters the arena, the enigmatic Jean Justice, along with his cohort, Jeremy Fox. Justice, unlike his partner Fox, was not a lawyer, having failed his bar exams, so may have had an axe to grind against the judicial system. He had rapidly evolved as a key Hanratty supporter, having been dismayed by the feeble case being presented against Hanratty and the apparent connivances on the part of the police and prosecution and quickly presented himself as a valiant knight leading a ground swell of opinion. Regarding Alphon as a much more villainous entity than Hanratty, he honed in on the susceptibilities of the unstable Alphon, whom had already courted publicity in relation to the "A6 Murder" – and the Dalal episode.

Although it cannot be denied that the pro-Hanratty lobby had plenty of sound arguments for protesting on Hanratty's behalf, along with highly respected exponents such as Paul Foot, exactly what motivated Jean Justice to spend a lifetime campaigning isn't entirely comprehendible; I would suggest that there was some element of personal gratification, in addition to any sense of injustice. Whatever, the root of his determination, he (along with Fox) took it upon himself to befriend Alphon, in the belief that he knew more about the "A6 Murder" than a completely innocent man should. Gradually, Alphon fed them what they wanted, but even they have admitted that much of what he claimed was simply not credible and/or could not be verified. There was also the matter of a financial incentive that had been advanced by Justice and co' in return for a full confession: though this ultimately was not forthcoming, mainly because Alphon continually blew hot and cold, it may have provided some impetus in drawing Alphon into the theatrical narrative. I believe Alphon simply said what he thought people wanted to hear in a bid to attract as much attention as possible. He even attempted to impose himself upon the Hanratty family; when they didn't reciprocate, he ended-up in fracas with them and assaulted Mrs Hanratty.

Alphon was both a witless lamb to the slaughter and a conniving miscreant all rolled into one.

Hidden within the 2002 Court of Appeal ruling [part 128] there is an extraordinary statement to the effect that the defence counsel [representing Hanratty's family] agreed that Peter Alphon could not have been the murderer and that this understanding resulted from the DNA evidence. This ostensibly puts to rest any involvement on the part of Alphon – or does it? It must now be accepted that he was not the gunman, but could he have had some conspiratorial roll? Alphon remained largely tight-lipped after 1971 and died in 2009 after a fall at home, so there is never going to be any deathbed confession or series of revelations. Janet Gregsten died in 1995, (coincidentally, in Horsham). Any suggestions of her involvement in a conspiracy to frighten or murder her husband have not gleaned the slightest hint of proof and (to anyone's knowledge) this avenue of enquiry has never even been entertained. Alphon had made various insinuations in respect to such a conspiracy, but they always fell on deaf ears as far as the authorities were concerned. Even Paul Foot eventually conceded that Alphon probably knew little, if anything.

However, despite the improbability of a conspiracy scenario, I don't think it can be completely ruled out and there might be a roll in that for Alphon that would perhaps explain a great deal about the case and his subsequent behaviour. So, I would like to propose one possible sequence of events, in which Alphon is one of the important protagonists.

Janet Gregsten, or someone close to her [with or without her knowledge], decides that the affair with Storie is an insult too far for his wife and children. Janet had been aware of her husband's previous philandering and the affair with Storie was a fairly open secret – she was just another one in a long catalogue of indiscretions. But everyone has their breaking point, including those whose sufferance is not direct. Let's imagine that someone acting on Janet Gregsten's behalf has some criminal contacts; there could be a whole chain of intermediaries. It is believed that Peter Alphon and Charles France were acquainted, though Alphon did not know Hanratty. Perhaps France acted as the central organiser and hired Alphon to do both reconnaissance and to construct an outline plan of when/where. The intention would be to scare Gregsten into ending the affair and transforming him into an eternally faithful husband. Hanratty was recruited to play the hoodlum.

Alphon, having made a study of the couple's movements over a period of a few weeks, identifies a perfect spot to ambush the couple. He had observed that when they visited the Old Station Inn [demolished c2001], which was just off the A4 heading into Slough, they would often go to Dorney Reach (approximately 3 miles away). He plans a date "to do the job". On the evening of 22 August 1961, Alphon goes to the Old Station Inn and waits for Gregsten and

Storie to arrive, then rings France (who is on standby).

Meanwhile, Hanratty, who though aware that he may be required that evening, decides to take a trip to Liverpool to sell some of his stolen jewellery, in the belief that it will be a quick transaction close to the railway station and he should be able to catch the train back in plenty of time. He first visits France to let him know his plans; during that conversation he mentions the Vienna Hotel as good place for Alphon to stay that night – Maida Vale is well away from any connection to them, (and of course, they always use false names).

Once in Liverpool, Hanratty realises that he's been on a wild goose chase and running out of time to get back to London, he opts to steal a car – something fast, like a Jaguar. At some point he rings France (at his usual haunt) to let him know the change of plan and that he can meet him close to Dorney Reach, rather than at Euston Station; they agree a location to rendezvous. France collects Alphon and they go to the meeting point agreed with Hanratty. Alphon takes the stolen car and dumps it in Maida Vale, then makes his way to the Vienna Hotel, having booked a room earlier in the day. France drives Hanratty to Dorney Reach and seeing the Morris minor is parked in the entrance to the cornfield he drops Hanratty off a little way up the road.

Hanratty has decided to use his gun [or has been given a gun for the "job"] to threaten the illicit couple; he's not had much chance to show it off, and having fired a few test shots to try it out, he found it makes him feel like a cowboy – like in the popular fifties American westerns. All Hanratty has to do is scare the living daylights out of the couple – possibly warn Gregsten to abandon his fornicating ways – steal their car, (leaving them stranded in the middle of a field,) then take the car into London and dump it: job done. Unfortunately, Hanratty gets other ideas and formulates an imaginative plan of his own...

After raping Storie, he concludes that he will now have to kill her, too. This is something he struggles with and hesitating, he distracts Storie while he thinks how to go about it; he asks her to explain how the car works – though, he knows perfectly well, really. He tells her to sit down next to Gregsten's dead body, still reluctant to finish it; she then surprises him by producing some money – he thought he had taken it all. As he begins to walk away, momentarily swayed by Storie's plea to leave her and go, he then abruptly grasps the nettle, turns and shoots. Unsure whether it's enough, he reloads and fires a few more shots; just to reassure himself, he kicks Storie's body: she appears to be dead. Hanratty carefully climbs into the car, ensuring no blood gets onto his clothes, before driving away at speed. Upon arriving at the outskirts of London, experiencing extreme fatigue, his head in turmoil, he decides to stop somewhere in order to rest and calm himself down; in the process he manages to ding the Morris at both ends. Eventually, he feels able to continue, though suffering considerable tiredness – he knows the city is waking up: he needs to get nearer home and dump the car before there are too many witnesses about. On reaching Redbridge, realising his driving is erratic, possibly drawing attention from increasing numbers of commuters, he finally abandons the car. Later he makes contact with France to let him know that the job has been completed, explaining that things hadn't quite gone to plan and would he dispose of the gun for him, which he hands him wrapped in his handkerchief, so as to avoid getting anyone's prints on it. Hanratty is advised to make his self scarce, so he returns to Liverpool, then later, Rhyl – there is no thought of a potential alibi at this stage: he just needs to lay low for a few days. France, meanwhile, meets up with Alphon in Maida Vale, taking the 36A bus and the opportunity to dispose of the weapon. A rather bewildered France conveys the bad news to Alphon, who enters a state of consternation and hides away at another hotel for the next few days. France succumbs to a deep sense of guilt and fear a few months later, committing suicide. Alphon comes to terms with the situation, banking on Hanratty not confessing all, with his neck on the line. Alphon and France would be manifestly aware that if they were implicated, they could face charges of conspiracy to murder and join Hanratty on the gallows. Equally, whoever set-up the job in the first place would be similarly at risk. Once the smoke clears, they all decide that Hanratty needs to take the fall and that bringing the police investigation to a close is in their best interests; the police are then anonymously tipped-off. The rest, as they say, is history. The former, is of course a fantasy – pure supposition. But, I hope that it does demonstrate that it is possible to make sense of a lot of the bizarre evidence in this case and construct at least one feasible scenario that corresponds with the known facts.

An interesting fact discovered by Paul Foot was the deposit of a very large sum of money into a bank account owned by Peter Alphon, around the beginning of 1962. The total amount was £7569, which was a very substantial sum of money in 1962, approximately equivalent to £147,000 in 2014 terms. Of this, £5000 could not be adequately explained and had been deposited in instalments. £5k is roughly £97k in 2014 terms. This is curious from several perspectives, because it indicates that Alphon was financially sound, possibly even before the murder. Why would he then need to acquire funds through criminal activity? The simply answer may be that he didn't. Nonetheless, the £5k is suspicious. But, that would have been an enormous amount of money to pay one intermediary in a conspiracy to just scare someone; in fact, it would seem excessive even to hire a murderer – returning to my little fantasy above though: buying someone's silence when the hangman's noose beckons, might encourage a *much* higher price. Alphon might just have been crazy enough to risk his own life to get that higher price and while he remained a high profile personality in the media, connected to the murder - even confessing to it – there would have been little danger of anyone eliminating him; not without stirring-up a hornet's nest of police suspicion. Perhaps by 1971, he felt safe. If this were true, it is not entirely conceivable that Alphon wouldn't know who ordered the "job", nor anything outside of his own brief, so could only speculate, albeit from an intimate angle. This could explain an awful lot about Alphon's behaviour and general involvement in the case following Hanratty's arrest.

Another mystery is how the cartridge cases were left at the Vienna Hotel. In answering this, it should be remembered that Hanratty was no 'Brain of Britain'; he regularly left fingerprints at the scenes of his burglaries – he was famous for it. If we bear in mind that at the stage when Hanratty was at the hotel, he was probably not envisaging firing the gun, let alone killing anyone, but had tried it out previously. He may have instinctively reloaded, without paying much importance to the spent cartridges – as highlighted earlier, used cartridge cases did not necessarily raise suspicion in 1961.

Wearing gloves may have been someone else's idea: France's, for example. He knew what Hanratty was like and would have wanted avoid any comeback from what was intended to be a relatively – albeit highly illegal – innocuous venture.

One further loose end was the death threats made against Valerie Storie while she was still in hospital. Many have suspected Alphon, which is certainly possible: it is the sort of thing one could imagine someone of Alphon's mischievous twisted personality being capable of, especially if we presume his involvement. Equally, this could have been just about any nutcase. In the Yorkshire Ripper case is a perfect example of how a seemingly normal average person could choose to create sickening taunts in letters and (most notably) the *Wearside Jack* tape, essentially out of boredom and, how high level police officers could be fooled into assigning credibility to hoax evidence – the consequence was that Sutcliffe was able to continue killing, while the police investigation ran into a blind alley. It shows that anyone can make a mistake and that no one can be unquestionably trusted. Whoever it was that made the threats against Storie, it is unlikely that it was the killer. However, harassment of Jean Justice (et al) and calls to newspapers *were* most likely the work of Alphon, irrespective of his involvement in the crime itself; he also took a rather unsavoury interest in Janet Gregsten. All in all, Alphon made quite a nuisance of himself.

There is one last peculiar detail to the case, which allegedly involved Janet Gregsten. On 19th February 1962, the *Daily Sketch* ran a front page story [the Daily Mail also ran one] claiming 8 days after the murder that Janet Gregsten had experienced a moment of psychic intuition while visiting an antique shop in Swiss Cottage [N. London]. She was accompanied by her brother-in-law [William Ewer, whom she later had an affair with] – the shop owner; they were trying to distract her thoughts from the terrible tragedy which had struck her, when quite suddenly she pointed out a man in the street [supposedly, Hanratty], saying: "That's the man the police are looking for." It should be noted that she had previously seen an identikit of the wanted man. According to the account, she not only believed he fitted the description, she had *sensed* it was him. She was sufficiently convincing in her assertion that Ewer later investigated. This man had been entering a cleaners' shop, where Ewer ascertained that he had given the name of 'J. Ryan' and an address in St John's Wood [NW London]. The next day Ewer was sitting in a cafe not far from his Antique shop (in Finchley Road) when he spotted the same man sitting nearby. When the man left, Ewer tried to follow him, but quickly lost track of him. Such was the man's closeness to the description and identikit of the gunman that Ewer contacted the police, who made enquiries at all the local shops in the vicinity. At a florists' it transpired that the man had ordered roses to be sent to Mrs Hanratty in Kingsbury – Hanratty was known to have sent flowers to his mother while on the run. However, at that stage, the police were not aware of any Jimmy Ryan, so they gave it no further attention. Ewer was determined not to be thwarted and regularly went out looking for the man for sometime afterward. During this period, he visited a business associate, one Louise Anderson. He discussed the "A6 Murder" with her, not knowing that Hanratty and Anderson were friends or that he had visited her shop that very morning... This was the gist of the story, all of which had led nowhere. The journalists involved swore blind that they had got this story from Ewer; certainly the details relating to Jimmy Ryan were found to be true, but Ewer and Janet Gregsten always vehemently denied that any of this episode ever occurred. This matter remains a mystery.

Regardless of how implausible one might consider the conspiracy theory explanation, it has been possible to (at least) imagine a hypothetical series of cohesive events that link much of the known facts and help shed light on some of the apparent anomalies of the case. Given that Alphon apparently knew France, while France was associated with Hanratty, who was connected to Anderson and that Anderson was associated with William Ewer – Janet Gregsten's brother-in-law and future lover – one surely has to wonder. How often the truth proves to be so much stranger than fiction. What really happened could be much simpler or complex than anyone could ever imagine. Apparent discrepancies may have simple solutions, while coincidences occur all the time. Most criminal cases do not get the amount of scrutiny and attention this one has and if there is some solid indisputable evidence, any anomalies or contradictions take on far less importance. In the final chapter I summarise all the salient points of the case (and few that have not yet been covered) in an attempt to put the whole case into some kind of clear cut perspective.

Chapter Five

The Final Analysis

The "A6 Murder" case is one of those that can never be wholly resolved to everyone's satisfaction. There are always going to be little loose ends that can't quite be neatly tied-up once and for all; this is an intrinsic element of historical cases and something that one simply has to accept as fundamentally inherent to them. Therefore, we should not seek or expect an immaculate resolution before permanently consigning this case to the criminal annals, just one that is adequately conclusive within the bounds of reasonable expectation. In this chapter I will effectively sum-up the pertinent incriminating material, placing the evidence into logical context; in addition, I will also confront a few of the outstanding issues affecting this case.

<u>The Case for the Prosecution</u>
(1) Hanratty fitted the description and identikit provided by Valerie Storie, who was the only witness that could have had a definite and non-fleeting glimpse of his face; she certainly recognised his eyes and was convinced of her identification. Hanratty was also cockney and would have had a reasonable familiarity with the outskirts of the North West of London, as exhibited by the gunman.

(2) Hanratty can be determined to have been able to be in Dorney Reach at the time the abduction began, regardless of whether he was in Liverpool that day or not.

(3) Hanratty was known to have stayed at the Vienna Hotel in Maida Vale on the night of the 21st August 1961, the night before the abduction. The fact that he stayed in Room 24 has never been disputed and it appears that only he could have left the spent cartridge cases in that room – those cases were definitively linked to the murder weapon.

(4) The .38 Enfield revolver used in the murder of Michael Gregsten and maiming of Valerie Storie was discovered behind the backseat of a Maida Vale route bus, wrapped in a used handkerchief, along with 60 rounds of ammunition; it would have had to be placed there sometime on the 23rd August. When the mucous contained in that handkerchief was analysed it was found to contain a single DNA profile which matched that of James Hanratty – the probability that this was not his DNA is exceedingly small. This proves that Hanratty had possession of the murder weapon within less than 18 hours of it being used at the crime scene. It is possible that an accomplice hid the gun on the bus, but it is probably not a coincidence that Hanratty (by his own admission) considered this a good place to dispose of unwanted stolen goods, or that he had very likely used this particular bus on a previous occasion.

(5) DNA identified from semen deposited on Valerie Storie's underwear also yielded a match with Hanratty's DNA profile, which seems to corroborate the handkerchief evidence.

(6) Hanratty's mental capacity was such that, though he was not necessarily pre-disposed to exhibit serious criminal behaviour, it was certainly not inconceivable. A significant head injury approximately 6 years prior to the committal of the crime could have been contributory to a pathological condition that might lead to psychotic or schizophrenic tendencies, and that in combination with his pre-existing demeanour had the potential to cause psychopathy.

(7) Hanratty's original alibi for the time of the abduction was unsubstantiatable from the outset, while his subsequent alibi was introduced very late on in the proceedings, despite there being no rational reason for not presenting that alibi initially. Although there are some apparent witnesses supporting the Rhyl alibi, they must be viewed with scepticism.

(8) Louise Anderson is claimed to have admitted that Hanratty did possess a gun and displayed a presumption of Hanratty's guilt. Why this evidence was not presented in court is unclear, but the person who conveyed this information had as much loyalty toward Hanratty as one would presume upon Anderson.

(9) The gunman was forensically identified as a blood Group A secretor, as was Hanratty. However, this blood group is representative of ca 40% of the British population. [NB: if the

number of potential suspects (as calculated in the Appendix) was 2.05 million, only ca 800,000 would have been Group A.]

(10) The gunman's supposed lack of driving ability is most likely a false deduction contrived in an effort to exonerate Hanratty who was an experienced driver – though unlikely to be a model one. This evidence must be regarded as inconclusive, but it should be noted that the gunman managed to drive from the Bedfordshire countryside to Redbridge at night, while undoubtedly in a very tired and agitated state.

(11) Hanratty's closest criminal associates gave evidence for the prosecution, but did display a reluctance to incriminate Hanratty. This could be construed as indicative of a struggle between their conscience and their loyalty to a friend (or possibly allegiance to a criminal code of silence).

(12) There were no other culpable suspects identified, either by the police or, indeed, *anyone* in the fifty plus years since the crime was committed.

Discrepancies and Distractions

(1) Peter Alphon's involvement was a major distraction and, unless considering him as having a possible supporting role in a conspiracy scenario, should now be completely dismissed as irrelevant.

(2) Possible planting of cartridge case evidence: clearly this still is a very important element of the case against Hanratty, so it is necessary to

address this insinuation. There is no logical reason why anyone in the criminal community would have set-up Hanratty, but it would have to have been part of the plan all along for that to be credible – which then leads into the conspiracy scenarios, which though possible, also don't really gel, unless we suppose that it was always the intention to kill the couple... At the time the cases were found, the Ryan/Hanratty connection either hadn't been made or certainly hadn't been firmly established, so there was no rational reason why the police might have conspired to strengthen a case against him; moreover, Alphon was still in the frame, so why not plant the evidence in Room 6? Nudds involvement is almost certainly completely incidental, and contraindicatively, he may well have attempted to frame Alphon; he did not need to change is original evidence in order to implicate Hanratty. There has been a suggestion that the hotel records were interfered with, but such accusations are tenuous and not entirely logical in the overall scheme of things.

(3) The Rhyl alibi witness evidence is problematic, but given the strength of the DNA evidence, which is more reliable?

(4) While Hanratty was in prison on remand awaiting trial, he allegedly made a confession to a fellow inmate, Roy Langdale. This does seem highly unlikely and everything about the account, including the fact that Langdale was a known prison "grass" infamous for lying to save his own skin at the expense of anyone, indicates that this is yet another red herring, which only

served to cast suspicion upon the police conduct. However, it is most likely that Langdale's information was not only pure invention, but one provided entirely of his own volition.

(5) Much has been made of the theatrical shenanigans of the Frances and Anderson during their court appearances by the pro-Hanratty lobby, implying that it was indicative of their own guilt, i.e. that they were coerced into giving misleading evidence. I would suggest the opposite was true and that they were struggling with their own complicity/conscience and an unwillingness to break the criminal code.

(6) During fifty years of investigation and campaigning by Hanratty's supporters, not one person has ever come forward to support any conspiracy or misconduct on the part of the police, nor has anyone ever presented any evidence that might indicate the involvement of anyone other than Hanratty – with the exception of Alphon.

(7) Hanratty was effectively sanitised into a mythical martyr because his family insisted he was "a nice bloke" and there was an unsustainably weak case made against him, riddled with dubious facets, which reeked of miscarriage of justice. But despite all of that, the fact remains that the jury still found him unanimously guilty. Meanwhile, an alternative evildoer was required, which conveniently presented itself as Peter Alphon, who unpleasant though probably he was, was even further demonised. In essence, the lynch mob

chased after someone who they thought looked a likely candidate, in the absence of any evidence [that they were willing to entertain] to the contrary.

(8) It is interesting background fact that Janet Gregsten and Valerie Storie have a different recollection of the number of times they had met prior to Michael Gregsten's murder. Janet recalled once, Valerie was convinced it was three times. Someone is either lying or has a very poor memory. If nothing else, it does go to prove that witness evidence, no matter how seemingly innocent, is just not reliable. But it is worth noting that despite there being no love lost between these two people, Janet showed an uncommon concern for Storie's medical welfare.

(9) Hanratty pleaded his innocence to the bitter end. While it is not unusual for criminals (in general) to deny their crimes, regardless of the evidence against them and to never confess, in Hanratty's case I believe that there is a simple reason for his reticence: he was deeply ashamed of the crime he had committed, and in particular, what was determined to be rape. He may have convinced himself the murder was an accident and that it wasn't actually rape, but he knew that no one else was ever going to accept that, especially not his mother – who would have been appalled had she allowed herself to concede her son's guilt. Hanratty could not face this, so a plea of diminished responsibility or any attempt at convincing the court that the murder

was accidental, in a bid to avoid the death penalty, was never going to be an option.

There is a final postscript to the case that might give hope to the Hanratty supporters. Assuming the DNA evidence to be unequivocal, is there any remaining possibility of Hanratty's innocence? Given that the underwear sample result is not definitive and there is some remote possibility of contamination in that instance, then the handkerchief sample must be regarded as the critical item of evidence – this sample was rediscovered in 1997 in an unsealed evidence bag. When Hanratty was arrested in 1961, he would most likely have been carrying a handkerchief, so the question has to be what became of that? Could it be possible that either, deliberately or accidentally, the handkerchief used to wrap the gun and the one Hanratty (presumably) had on him at arrest, become swapped? Realistically, it doesn't seem likely that this would happen accidentally, which therefore means that we would have to suppose that it would be a deliberate act. In 1961/2 and (logically) until the early 1990's, there would not have been any forensically sound reason to make such a swap. But, by 1997, DNA profiling was an established tool, though still not sensitive enough to enable analysis of samples of very low yield; nonetheless, it would have been known, or at least anticipated that techniques were being developed that could be sufficiently sensitive, such that at some point it would be possible to derive a profile from the handkerchief sample. It is a very long stretch of one's credulity, but it is possible that the samples could have been swapped in or around 1997. This does require a number of provisos however: (i) that this other Hanratty sample existed, survived and was identifiable, (ii) that someone would have been motivated to make the swap in order to ensure [or in hope of ensuring] that Hanratty was proved to be guilty, (iii) that such person would have had the opportunity to make that swap. It is difficult to imagine who would have the motive, especially combined with the means, to execute such a deception, particularly given that even the police had long been of the opinion that Hanratty was innocent. In conclusion: a highly implausible scenario, but not an impossible one. I don't personally believe in this, I simply pose it hypothetically, so as to cover all the bases.

Of course, hindsight is wonderful thing. Had the DNA evidence been available in 1961/2 then, presuming the result would have been the same, the "A6 Murder" case would most probably have never attracted such an abundance of controversy, and although it would still have been a shocking case at the time, it also most probably would not have attained the same level of infamy. The advocates of common justice and judicial reform would not have been nearly so driven to defend Hanratty; and had the death penalty not been administered, there would have been far less unease.

The removal of capital punishment from the criminal statute book in 1965 was perhaps an understandable reaction to cases such as the "A6 Murder". However, in the intervening 50 years, forensic techniques have advanced enormously, DNA profiling has added an extra dimension to identification and evidence handling procedures are now extremely rigorous. The possibility of miscarriages of justice has been exponentially reduced. Personally, I would support the reintroduction of the death penalty for certain extreme crimes, provided that proper safeguards are incorporated and, only when the evidence is considered to have attained a particularly high level of probability. Inevitably, any form of execution will evoke vociferous human rights driven interventionism, but this should not circumvent the right of the populous to choose a system of punishment that satisfies the need for ultimate retribution in certain circumstances. And let us not forget that Hanratty was guilty after all.

I would strongly advise readers to consult Paul Foot's and Bob Woffinden's excellent books in order to fully appreciate the background and complexities of this case. These books are openly biased towards Hanratty's innocence, but they are the most comprehensively accessible sources; it is also worth reading the 2002 Court of Appeal ruling, which is freely available on the internet.

Epilogue

This case boils down to two issues: the DNA evidence and the Rhyl alibi. These two pieces of evidence cannot be reconciled; they cannot both be true. If one accepts the DNA evidence, Hanratty was guilty. If one dismisses the DNA and accepts the Rhyl alibi, Hanratty was innocent. The Rhyl alibi depends on unreliable witness testimony; the DNA evidence depends on uncontaminated samples.

One potential question remains: if not Hanratty, then who else?

References

'Who Killed Hanratty?'
by Paul Foot (1973) [ISBN-13: 978-0586038130].

'Hanratty: The Final Verdict'
by Bob Woffinden (1999) [ISBN-13: 978-0330353014].

England and Wales Supreme Court of Judicature – Court of Appeal (Criminal Division); Regina v James Hanratty (deceased)...
[web addresses:
http://www.bailii.org/ew/cases/EWCA/Crim/2002/1141.html, or
http://www.denverda.org/DNA_Documents/Hanratty.PDF].

Wikipedia website
[web address:
http://en.wikipedia.org/wiki/James_Hanratty].

Mail Online article from 2001
[web address:
http://www.dailymail.co.uk/news/article-35427/DNA-tests-Hanratty-guilty.html].

Mail Online article from 2002
[web address:
http://www.dailymail.co.uk/news/article-113967/Hanratty-victim-vindicated.html].

BBC Home (Beds, Herts & Bucks) online article from 2009
[web address:
http://www.bbc.co.uk/threecounties/content/articl es/2009/04/08/crime_hanratty_murder_feature.s html].

Cover Image

Eagle-eyed experts may have noted that the vehicle depicted on the book cover is in fact a slightly later model of Morris Minor to the one owned by Gregsten; his car also had a split screen. Nonetheless, it is representative of the time. The gun in the cover image is certainly the correct type: it is therefore presumed that it must be very similar to the actual murder weapon.

Appendix

Calculation of DNA Profile Matching Probability (estimate)

The data sources used in this estimation are freely available on the internet. It should be realised that global ethnicity distribution was derived from data collated since 2000 and as such is only an estimate of the current value and it is assumed that the 1961 value would be within 2% of this value, rounded down to provide a minimum sample size – this reduces the matching probability and is therefore a cautious value.

SGM+ (Second Generation Multiplex Plus) is the profiling system used for the UK National DNA Database since 1998. This relies on 10 STR's (Short Tandem Repeats) which theoretically supports a matching probability of 1 in 10 million million. However, a value of *1 in 1000 million* [i.e. a billion] is considered to be statistically supportable. Therefore, to statistically find 2 people at random with the same DNA profile (using this test) would be 1 in a billion given a sample size of 2 billion. For comparison, the current global population is estimated at just over 7 billion. So, if this test were applied to every human currently on the face of the Earth, the chances that 2 randomly chosen individuals would have an identical DNA profile would be 1 in 285.7 million.

Based on the 1961 Census:
The Male Population of England = 21 million (approx);

Males aged between 20 – 39 in England & Wales = 6 million (approx); this represented 13% (approx) of the total population. Assuming this value to be representative of England alone, then the total number of males aged 20 – 39 in England in 1961 = **2.73 million** (approx).

The total population of Greater London in 1961 = 7.78 million (which represented 37% of the total population of England); based on this value, I have chosen to include 75% of the male population of England in 1961 in the *A6 Murder* sample. This equates to a total of **2.05 million** potential suspects that can be realistically included.

Assuming that the ethnicity of England in 1961 was approx. 100% European [the ethnically white population of England in 2011 was approx. 90%, but in 1961 this figure would have been close to 100%] and that the European ethnicity represented 10% of the world population in 1961 [Approx. 11.4% in circa 2000.] – which is a probable underestimate – then I have assumed that the European genome type is representative of 10% of the statistically possible 1 billion DNA profile variations [taken from above].

In conclusion, there are **100 million** possible DNA profile variants relevant to this case. Given a total sample population of 2.05 million [and the chances of 2 people at random having the same

DNA profile is 1 in 100 million for a 200 million sample population] then the probability that Hanratty's DNA would be a random match to another individual would be **1 in 10 billion**.

The total global population in 1960 has been estimated at 3 billion.